EMILIE DAVIS'S CIVIL WAR

EMILIE DAVIS'S

Civil War

THE DIARIES OF A FREE BLACK WOMAN
IN PHILADELPHIA, 1863–1865

EDITED BY
Judith Giesberg

TRANSCRIBED AND ANNOTATED BY
The Memorable Days Project Editorial Team

THE PENNSYLVANIA STATE UNIVERSITY PRESS
UNIVERSITY PARK, PENNSYLVANIA

Frontispiece: Portrait of two young African American women (detail), ca. 1870–1900. Anthony Barboza Collection, LC-USZ62-136919. Library of Congress Prints and Photographs Division, Washington, D.C.

Library of Congress Cataloging-in-Publication Data

Davis, Emilie Frances, 1838–1899, author.
Emilie Davis's Civil War : the diaries of a free Black woman in Philadelphia, 1863-1865 / edited by Judith Giesberg ; transcribed and annotated by the Memorable Days Project Editorial Team.
        pages   cm
Summary: "A transcription and annotation of the diary of Emilie Davis, a free African American woman who lived in Philadelphia during the Civil War"—Provided by publisher.
Includes bibliographical references and index.
ISBN 978-0-271-06367-6 (cloth : alk. paper)
ISBN 978-0-271-06368-3 (pbk. : alk. paper)
1. Davis, Emilie Frances, 1838-1899—Diaries.
2. African American women—Pennsylvania—Philadelphia—Diaries.
3. African Americans—Pennsylvania—Philadelphia—History—19th century.
4. Philadelphia (Pa.)—History—Civil War, 1861–1865.
5. Philadelphia (Pa.)—Social conditions—19th century.
6. Philadelphia (Pa.)—Race relations—History—19th century.
I. Giesberg, Judith Ann, 1966- editor. II. Memorable Days Project Editorial Team, transcriber. III. Title.

F158.44.D38 2014
974.8'1103092—dc23
[B]
2013049318

THE MEMORABLE DAYS PROJECT EDITORIAL TEAM

Judith Giesberg

Theresa Altieri

Rebecca Capobianco

Thomas Foley

Ruby Johnson

Jessica Maiberger

To Emilie, who taught us so much.

CONTENTS

INTRODUCTION

Emilie Davis's Civil War

1

1863

1864

1865

CODA

All's Well that Ends Well

195

ILLUSTRATIONS

ACKNOWLEDGMENTS

This book started as a class project: each member of my spring 2012 graduate seminar looked at a section of Emilie Davis's diary for what it might have to say about the Civil War. The enthusiastic response from these students encouraged a small group of us to pursue the project into the summer. Jacqueline (Jackie) Beatty, Timothy English, Michael Fiorelli, Brent Freedland, Matt Landis, Colin McNulty, Molly Rigas, Ryan Sheridan, and Kelly Smith were among the first to advocate on Emilie's behalf and each helped make this book possible. Three of the five student members of the Memorable Days Project editorial team—Thomas (Tom) Foley, Jessica (Jess) Maiberger, and Theresa Altieri—were among these early friends of Emilie, and they recruited Rebecca (Becca) Capobianco and Ruby Johnson. Early on, Jess exhibited an extraordinary ability to read Emilie's small and often faded handwriting, and she patiently taught the rest of us how to see. I don't know that we would have continued had it not been for Jess. All through the following summer, Tom, Jess, Theresa, and Becca finished transcribing and annotating the diary, even though Theresa and Jess had already graduated. Ruby joined us in the fall, and Michael Mafodda had signed on to be our web designer and guru.

We owe Michael Mafodda special thanks for making possible Emilie's debut in the form of the Memorable Days website (http://www.davisdiaries.villanova.edu), for teaching us HTML, and for patiently fixing all the things we broke. Support for constructing the site came from Villanova faculty and staff and the offices they oversee, including Laura Bang, Michael Foight, Marc Gallicchio, Maurice Hall, David Lacy, Joe Lucia, Kathleen Scavello, David Uspal, and Carol Weiss. Jean Ann Linney, Dean of Arts and Sciences, and Father Peter Donohue, O.S.A., University President, took special interest in this project, which we deeply appreciate. Ms. Christine Filiberti looked after all history graduate students, and she made sure those involved in this project were paid and fed. We miss Chris.

Early comments on the website and from teachers whose classes we visited—including Terry Canny, Tom Rendulich, Michael Burkhimer, Kimberly Carroll, and Erika Grimminger—convinced us that we should publish Emilie's diaries as a book. At Penn State, William Blair encouraged us to pursue the work and, through his People's Contest project (http://www.peoplescontest.psu.edu), he made digitized copies of the diary pages available. Penn State University Press was our first choice for publishing the book, and Kathryn Yahner and Charlee Redman have been enthusiastic and supportive. Laura Reed-Morrisson at the Press read the entire manuscript with a keen eye, catching words we missed in the transcription and suggesting new annotations. Special thanks to Christopher H. Hayashida-Knight, a Penn State PhD candidate, for sharing a find about Emilie's family.

I would like to thank my generous history department colleagues Marc Gallicchio, Jeff Johnson, Catherine Kerrison, Paul Rosier, Paul Steege, and Mark Sullivan for their thoughtful comments and recommendations on the introduction and for helping me think through the organization of the book. Jill Lepore (Harvard University) delivered a splendid lecture at Villanova on Jane Franklin and afterward encouraged me to enlist my students in finding out more about Emilie. Randall Miller (St. Joseph's University) and J. Matthew Gallman (University of Florida) read the entire manuscript with great care, provided thoughtful advice and guidance, and gently corrected our mistakes. Without Matt's and Randall's work on Philadelphia in the Civil War, we would not have attempted a project like this. Early exchanges with Karsonya (Kaye) Wise Whitehead (University of Maryland, Baltimore County) and Constance Cole helped us ask the right questions about the diary and the people mentioned in it. Nicole Joniec at the Library Company of Philadelphia and Hillary Kativa at the Historical Society of Pennsylvania knew just where to look for illustrations; Patrick Madden (Villanova MA student) and Leslie Willis (Temple University Libraries) helped track down the rest, and funding from Suzanne Smeltzer and the members of Villanova's subventions committee helped cover the permissions costs.

Thank you to Villanova University's Joanne Quinn and David Uspal for their work on the map of Emilie's neighborhood and to Menika Dirkson (Villanova MA student) and Edward Fierros for their help with the photographs in Chapter 1. Three other MA students—Michael Johnson, Joanna Voortman, and Eileen Brumitt—assisted as well. Michael and Joanna read and corrected citations and pointed out other mistakes that needed addressing, and Eileen helped prepare the index.

Collaborating with my students on the Memorable Days Project has been *the* most rewarding work I have done as a college professor. Ruby, Tom, Becca, and I spent many long hours together exploring Emilie's Civil War diaries, and the three of them then traveled around the mid-Atlantic region, introducing Emilie to teachers, bloggers, reporters, radio and television audiences, university alumni, community activists, and anyone else who would listen. I owe each of them an enormous debt of gratitude for reminding me why I love teaching, and I look forward to watching each of them take inspiration from their own students.

Judith Giesberg
Havertown, Pennsylvania

ROBERT AND MARY ADGER

A former slave, Robert Adger became a successful furniture dealer in Philadelphia. Robert and his wife, Mary, lived in the Seventh Ward, where the couple raised thirteen children. Robert and Mary's son William graduated from the Institute for Colored Youth (ICY) and became the first African American graduate of the University of Pennsylvania.

CHARLES BUSTILL

The Bustill family was prominent in Philadelphia. Charles Bustill was a plasterer and an Underground Railroad conductor. Charles and his wife, Emily, had two daughters, Louisa and Gertrude—nine and eight, respectively, in 1863. Also living in the Bustill household was a Caroline Fisher; see the entry for "Nell/Nellie" below.

OCTAVIUS CATTO

A son of William Catto, Octavius Catto was a teacher at the ICY and co-founder, with Jacob C. White Jr., of the Pythians baseball club. Catto was active in the Banneker Institute, an African American literary society, and he was among the recruits who volunteered to defend Pennsylvania in June 1863 during the Confederate invasion.

WILLIAM CATTO

The father of Octavius, William Catto was a minister at the First African Presbyterian Church. William Catto was a founding member of the Banneker Institute and a close associate of Jacob C. White Sr., who directed the Sunday school at Catto's church.

ALFRED DAVIS

Born in 1833, Emilie's brother Alfred Davis was thirty years old in 1863. In 1850, Alfred lived with his father, Isaac, in Pottsville,

Pennsylvania, where they both worked as waiters. Alfred and his wife, Mary, had a son, Frank ("Little Frank"), in 1857. Alfred mustered into the U.S. Navy in October 1863 and served on the USS *Mount Vernon*.

ELIJAH (EJ) DAVIS

Emilie's brother Elijah Davis, or EJ, was born in Maryland in 1820, making him approximately forty-three years old in 1863. EJ's wife, Sarah Davis, was twenty-eight years old in 1863, and the couple had one son, Elwood, who was three at that time. EJ settled in Philadelphia in 1844. In 1860, EJ lived at 916 Rodman Street, and in 1862 he resided at 1039 Lombard Street, both located in the Seventh Ward. Like Emilie's job as a servant, Elijah Davis's occupation as a "waiter" is consistent with the limited work prospects available to women and men of color in the antebellum North.

ELWOOD (LITTLE ELWOOD) DAVIS

Elwood, also referred to as Little Elwood, was the son of Elijah and Sarah Davis. Three years old in 1863, Elwood was Emilie's nephew.

EMILIE F. DAVIS

Emilie F. Davis was twenty-four years old in 1863. According to the 1860 census, Emilie worked as a servant, and she lived with family members Elijah (EJ, her brother), Sarah (EJ's wife), Elwood (EJ and Sarah's son), Elizabeth, and Thomas Davis. By 1863, she was living on her own. Emilie mentions a number of members of her family, including her father, Isaac; brothers Alfred and Elijah; her sister, Anne; and various members of their families. Emilie was a student at the ICY, and she attended church serves at the Seventh Street Presbyterian Church, also known as the First (Colored) Presbyterian Church, on Seventh Street below Shippen. Emilie cared for children, sewed, and completed other tasks related to her work as a domestic servant.

FRANK (LITTLE FRANK) DAVIS

Frank Davis was Emilie's nephew and was approximately seven years old in 1863. His father, Alfred, joined the U.S. Navy, and after his mother, Mary Davis, died, Frank's uncle, Elijah, surrendered custody of the boy to the Association for the Care of Colored Orphans, a Quaker-run orphanage.

ISAAC DAVIS
Isaac Davis, Emilie's father, was approximately sixty-three years old in 1863. Isaac lived in Harrisburg, Pennsylvania, with Anne and Levi Friver—perhaps his daughter and son-in-law—and their son, Levi Jr. Isaac was born in Maryland. Nothing is known of Emilie's mother.

AUNT JANE (DAVIS)
Two women listed in the 1860 census might be Emilie's Aunt Jane. One Jane Davis (who lived alone in the Fourteenth Ward) was eighty-seven years old in 1860. Another Jane Davis lived with Joseph and Mary Boland in the Fifth Ward; she was seventy years old in 1860. Both women were listed as "colored." The younger of the two is ten years older than Emilie's father, Isaac, making her perhaps the likelier candidate.

MARY DAVIS
Approximately twenty-five years old in 1863, Mary was married to Alfred Davis and had a son, Frank (Little Frank), who was seven years old at the time. Mary was Emilie's sister-in-law.

SARAH DAVIS
Sarah Davis was twenty years old in 1863, married to Elijah Davis, and mother to Elwood, the couple's son, who was three years old at the time. Emilie's sister-in-law, Sarah served as treasurer of the Ladies' Union Association in 1865.

THOMAS (TOM, TOMY) DAVIS
Thomas also lived with Elijah Davis in 1860. In 1862, Tomy was fourteen years old; he enlisted in the U.S. Navy and served on the USS *Cimarron*.

JONATHAN C. GIBBS

Jonathan C. Gibbs was the pastor of the Seventh Street Presbyterian Church, also known as the First (Colored) Presbyterian Church. Emilie mentions Reverend Gibbs several times, including in March 1865 when he left the church to establish schools and minister to southern freedpeople. Formally separated from the First (Colored) Presbyterian in 1866, Gibbs was elected to the Florida Constitutional Convention in 1868. He served as state superintendent of public education and as Florida's secretary of state—the first African American to serve in this capacity.

INSTITUTE FOR COLORED YOUTH (ICY)

Founded by Quakers in 1837, the Institute for Colored Youth was a coeducational preparatory high school for African Americans. The primary focus of the institute was to train African Americans as teachers; the school admitted boys and girls, offering students a rigorous curriculum of classical languages, science, and mathematics. Although the original funds were provided by white Quakers, the ICY was staffed and run by men and women of color.

LADIES' UNION ASSOCIATION (LUA)

The Ladies' Union Association was founded in July 1863 to raise money and provide supplies for the sick and wounded USCT; their efforts included a trip up the Delaware River to deliver supplies to a USCT hospital in Bristol, Pennsylvania, in June 1865. In February 1865, the Association reorganized to work on behalf of the recently emancipated freedmen. Caroline LeCount, an ICY graduate and teacher, served as corresponding secretary. Emilie's sister-in-law, Sarah Davis, served as treasurer of the LUA in 1865. The Ladies' Union Association enjoyed considerable success as it raised money among members of Philadelphia's African American community and helped end the city's streetcar segregation.

NELL/NELLIE

We have been unable to identify Nell or Nellie, but she was either Emilie's sister or a very close friend. Although "Nell" might be shorthand for Cornelia, Danielle, or Eleanor, two Carolines also figure prominently in the diary. One, Caroline E. White, was married to Jacob C. (Jake) White Jr. She was born in Virginia in 1828, and the census describes her as a "sales lady." The other, Caroline Fisher, lived with the Charles Bustill family and was sixteen years old in 1863.

SOCIAL, CIVIL, AND STATISTICAL ASSOCIATION OF THE COLORED PEOPLE OF PENNSYLVANIA

The Social, Civil, and Statistical Association of the Colored People of Pennsylvania was founded in 1860 to combat racism, violence, and prejudice against members of the African American community of Philadelphia. The association's membership consisted of many prominent black Philadelphians. During the war years, the association hosted frequent lectures, attracting black and white orators alike, including Frederick Douglass, Rev. James Sella Martin, Frances Ellen Watkins Harper, and Philadelphia judge and Republican congressman William D. Kelley. Octavius Catto and other institution members organized black Philadelphians to push for the end of discrimination on the city's streetcars.

GEORGE BUSTILL WHITE

George Bustill White was a son of Jacob C. White Sr.—a prominent black businessman—and Elizabeth White. During the Civil War, the White family included seven adult children: Elizabeth, George, Jacob (Jake) Jr., Henry, Martin, Joseph, and Sarah. George attended the ICY and was active in the Banneker Institute.

JACOB C. (JAKE) WHITE JR.

Jacob C. (Jake) White Jr. was a son of Jacob C. White Sr. and Elizabeth White. The Whites were a prominent black family that, during the Civil War, included seven adult children: Elizabeth, George, Jacob (Jake) Jr., Henry, Martin, Joseph, and Sarah. Like his brother George, Jacob attended the ICY and was active in the Banneker Institute. In April 1864, White became principal of the Roberts Vaux Primary School. White co-founded the Pythians, a black baseball team, with Octavius Catto. He married Caroline E. White, possibly Emilie's friend Nellie.

A NOTE ON METHOD

Emilie Davis wrote in a clear and proficient hand. In transcribing her diaries, the Memorable Days editorial team strove to preserve as much of the original form of the entries as we thought possible. Toward that end, we have added no punctuation and made very few spelling interventions. Readers will note that, because of the limited space allotted for each day, Davis's daily entries often carry over into the next day. We decided to leave them that way, as it is clear enough to readers when Emilie has finished a thought, even if she did not think to add punctuation for the convenience of modern readers.[1] Like many of her contemporaries, Davis's spelling is idiosyncratic, and she often shortened words, perhaps to fit them into the limited space. Modern readers familiar with the shorthand used by twenty-somethings in their texts and tweets will perhaps not find any of this surprising. With a few exceptions, we have preserved Davis's spelling; when we made a spelling intervention we did so in brackets, as on June 20, 1863, when we added "[war]" when the original word looks like "ware," and on July 8, 1863, when we added "[Cape May]."

Despite our very best efforts, words and passages remain illegible. After May 29, 1864, Emilie wrote many of her entries in pencil, and the writing on some of these pages is blurred and faded. When we could not read something, we indicate the missing word or words with a bracketed ellipsis. The most difficult words to read were often proper names, and the difficulty in reading them was compounded by the use of nicknames or initials. Interested readers are encouraged to go to the Memorable Days website, http://www.davisdiaries.villanova.edu, where they can read the original diary pages and help us continue to identify the people mentioned in the diary.

1. Linguists may find in the rhythm of Emilie's private writing evidence of vernacular culture and other clues about her family history that we historians have been unable to learn from the records Emilie left behind. On African American language as a "resistance discourse," see Smitherman, *Word from the Mother*; on "Black English Vernacular" and its potential regional differences, see Labov, *Language in the Inner City*.

The team was keenly aware that in annotating, we were making assumptions and creating our own narrative that would parallel the text of the diary. Readers of our annotations will note our use of conditional verbs such as "may have" and "likely was," and we trust they will recognize in this language the uncertainty that remains part of studying subjects with a narrow source base. Because we did not want our own voices to talk over Emilie's original intentions, we generally chose to annotate when we thought readers would benefit from the context or when we hoped an annotation would help them make a connection that would have been clear to Emilie or her contemporaries, had she shared her diary with them. We also hope the annotations will encourage some to keep reading to learn more about the Civil War, even when they suspect that Emilie has forgotten about it. In the end, we have a hunch that what modern readers might mistake for Emilie's forgetting the war is really the war's saturation in all parts of her life—in the meetings she attends, the discussions she has with classmates and friends, and in the encounters she has on the streets of her neighborhood. We might forget about *our* wars some days, but it is unlikely that Civil War Americans did so as easily or readily—particularly when friends and family were fighting and dying in it. We hope the annotations communicate this.

Like all scholars working in microhistory, we are aware of the dangers that come with identifying too strongly with our subject—of "falling in love," as Jill Lepore has so aptly put it. We like to think we avoided this pitfall, but if pushed, some of us might admit to having an alter ego among Emilie's circle of friends and family. None of us would claim to *be* Emilie, but among us there is a classmate, trusted friend, concerned sibling, and teacher. As an exercise in microhistory, we have sought to trace our "elusive subject" through the few records she left behind, tried to solve "small mysteries," and made a case for how knowing Emilie helps us get closer to understanding the meaning of the Civil War.[2] Now we invite our readers to help us solve the remaining mysteries.

The Memorable Days Project Editorial Team

---

2. Lepore, "Historians Who Love Too Much," 133, 141.

Introduction: Emilie Davis's Civil War

Emilie Davis lived through America's transition from slavery to freedom, but as a young, working-class woman of color, she left only faint traces of herself in the official records. Davis appeared in three consecutive censuses, beginning in 1860. Her 1866 marriage was recorded in a Philadelphia marriage registry; when Emilie died in 1889, at age fifty, a physician and an undertaker affixed their signatures to her death certificate.[1] She was twenty-two years old, free, and living in a free state in 1861. The Civil War did not promise to change her legal status, nor would enlistment offer her the opportunity to prove her mettle. Indeed, it might seem that Emilie Davis had very little at stake in the war. Emilie was married soon after the war ended, had five children, and was buried in a grave that is no longer marked.[2] Davis seems to offer us little that we did not already know about the Civil War, and she did not leave us much to go on. We might have easily gone on without her—except that she kept a diary.

1. George Bustill White and Emily [*sic*] Frances Davis, December 13, 1866, Return of Marriages, October 22–December 31, 1866, Philadelphia City Archives. "Pennsylvania, Philadelphia City Death Certificates, 1803–1915," index and images, FamilySearch, https://familysearch.org/pal:/MM9.1.1/J6S3-9L6 (accessed May 10, 2013), Emily F. White, 1889.

2. 1880 United States Federal Census, Philadelphia, Pennsylvania, roll 1173, family history film 1255173, page 10C, enumeration district 197, image 0022. Census information throughout this volume derives from the online database maintained by Ancestry.com and The Church of Jesus Christ of Latter-Day Saints, Provo, Utah.

FIGURE I Emilie Davis's 1863 diary. With limited space available for Emilie to make her daily entries, she often continued writing into the next day's lines and filled the memoranda pages at the back of each volume. Emilie Davis diary, 1863 (DAMS 1418), vol. 1 of Davis diaries [3030], Historical Society of Pennsylvania. Photo: Edward Fierros and Menika Dirkson.

Like so many of the Civil War generation, Emilie recorded these memorable days in her diary. She wrote short daily entries, recounting events both big and small, in three slim pocket-sized volumes. A seamstress by trade, she reported on her sewing work; keeping the diary allowed Emilie to practice her handwriting as she attended school at the Institute for Colored Youth, Philadelphia's premier African American school. Immersed in the lively social life of the city's black community, Emilie used her diary to keep track of her social calls and correspondence, and in its pages she repeated gossip and rumors about derailed courtships and marriages gone wrong. Mixed in with the minutiae of Emilie's everyday life are entries recounting black Philadelphians' celebration of the Emancipation Proclamation, nervous excitement during the battle of Gettysburg, and their collective mourning of President Lincoln. Indeed, on the first line of the earliest surviving diary, under the heading "Thursday, January 1, 1863," Emilie writes,

> *To day has bin a memorable day and i thank god i have bin sperd [spared] to see it the day was religously observed all the churches were open we had quite a Jubiliee in the evenin i went to Joness to a Party had a very pleasant time*[3]

Entries like this one make the diary and its author worth a closer look.

If we mine Davis's 381-page diary for events we deem *newsworthy* about the Civil War, we might learn a thing or two about what the war looked like through the eyes of a free black woman. In this way, Emilie Davis's frank and descriptive diary entries serve as bracing counterpoints to the commentary provided by the smug New York diarist George Templeton Strong, for instance, or entries carefully crafted by the self-conscious and indignant Mary Boykin Chesnut of Charleston. Commenting on the initial proclamation, Strong remarked cynically in his diary that it would "do us good abroad, but will have no other effect."[4] Like Davis, Chesnut celebrated emancipation—but for starkly different reasons. A fierce critic of slavery, Chesnut despised slavery's effect on white women, declaring in her diary that only "Lincoln's proclamation freeing the negroes" could

---

3. Emilie Davis Diary, January 1–3, 1863, Historical Society of Pennsylvania, Philadelphia (HSP).

4. Strong, *Diary of George Templeton Strong*, 262.

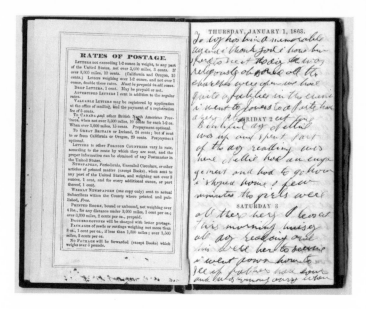

FIGURE 2   Diary page for January 1, 1863. On the first page of her diary, Emilie described celebrations held in honor of the Emancipation Proclamation. Emilie Davis diary, 1863 (DAMS 1418), Emilie Davis diaries [3030], vol. 1, Historical Society of Pennsylvania.

reconcile her to a Confederate defeat.[5] Philadelphia diarist and lawyer Sydney George Fisher was uncharacteristically effusive when, in a long and ponderous reflection on the constitutionality of wartime emancipation, he declared, "we should try to enlarge our vision so as to see the real dimensions of things around us, which dwarf all of our past experience."[6] Only in Emilie's diary is January 1 a "Jubiliee," and neither Strong, nor Chesnut, nor Fisher saw God's work in emancipation. The women of Philadelphia's Female Anti-Slavery Society rejoiced, welcoming "the Day of Jubilee which has dawned

5. Chesnut, *Mary Chesnut's Civil War*, 407.

6. "The President's Proclamation of September 22," *North American and United States Gazette*, November 29, 1862, 1. In an entry from January 1, 1860, Fisher declared slavery "a moral wrong," yet his diary reveals little of his own thinking about emancipation—and, three years later, he made no mention of the significance of the new year. See Fisher, *Philadelphia Perspective*, January 1, 1860, 343.

on the American Nation."[7] Participating in celebrations among freed-people and colored troops in South Carolina, fellow Philadelphian and freedmen's teacher Charlotte Forten declared, "a happy, happy New Year to you, too! And to us all a year of such freedom as we have never yet known in this boasted but hitherto wicked land."[8] Through Davis's eyes, readers are reminded that free blacks embraced emancipation as the beginning of the end of a painful duality—of being half citizens in a slave nation.

But if we extracted these big events from the diary, we would be no closer to knowing its author. The real significance of the diary is that it allows us to see how the Civil War was lived as part of everyday life, folded between Emilie's sewing and her attendance at church and school, shopping and socializing, worrying and rejoicing. We generally *study* the war as a series of big events, of victories and setbacks, turning points and proclamations, but it was *lived* as a periodic and oftentimes unwelcome visitor, taking at times and giving at others. Emilie Davis's diary gives us a sense of the war as a dramatic interruption of life in a northern city.

Reading the diary, one is struck by the uneven pace in which the Civil War was experienced. Entries focused on the weather, Emilie's work, and her social life feel slow and will likely make some readers impatient for war news. Emilie, too, became impatient, as in June 1863, when she heard that the rebels had entered Pennsylvania and were headed to Harrisburg, where her father lived. On June 23, Emilie writes, "i feel so worried about Father." Six days later, with refugees from Harrisburg crowded in the streets of Philadelphia, Emilie's concern is palpable when she writes, "i sent a letter to Father last night." By June 30, Emilie is "all most sick worrin about father." Following this entry, Emilie continues to report war news without giving voice to her mounting concerns. Finally, on July 9, Davis writes with relief, "i received a liter from Father."[9] Although we think of Gettysburg as a three-day battle, full of low- and high-water marks

---

7. The Philadelphia Female Anti-Slavery Society (PFASS), Minutes 1833–1870, HSP, January 8, 1863.

8. Grimké, *Journals*, 434.

9. Davis Diary, June 23, 29, 30 and July 9, 1863.

and events occurring in rapid succession, in the pages of Emilie's diary, it becomes a three-week grind of rumors and worry.

April 1865 entries, on the other hand, remind us that events also happened quickly, and news traveled with dizzying speed. On April 14, Emilie attends a "Parrade" to celebrate the raising of the U.S. flag at Fort Sumter and to honor the 24th Regiment of United States Colored Troops (USCT) from Camp William Penn. Then, on the morning of April 15, while at a meeting of the Ladies' Union Association—an organization that raised money and supplies for the USCT—Emilie learns the "very sad newes" that the president had been shot. Later that day, Emilie turns to the miscellaneous pages in the back of her diary, where she adds additional information she must have learned since the morning. Lincoln was assassinated, she reports, by "Som Confederate villain at the theathre." Lincoln died early Saturday morning, and Emilie reports that "the city is in the Deepest sorrow." Readers can imagine how disorienting it must have been for Emilie to watch her city go from celebration to mourning within twenty-four hours. Like her fellow black Philadelphians, Lincoln's death left Emilie with a sense of unease, which she expresses rather succinctly: "These are strang times."[10] One of the extraordinary things about Emilie Davis's diaries is that they can make the Civil War seem strange to us again; they allow readers to relive these memorable days without knowing the outcome.

Although she was born free, Emilie Davis's early years were shaped by slavery. Emilie's father, Isaac Davis, had a son, Elijah, in Maryland in 1820 and then made his way to Pennsylvania some time before the birth of his son Alfred in 1833 and Emilie in 1839. (Anne Friver, with whom Isaac lived, was perhaps Isaac's second child; she was born in Pennsylvania in 1826.) Whether there were other children, we do not know; gone too is information about Isaac's wife and the mother of his children. Isaac's status when he first arrived in Pennsylvania is also unclear. Indentured labor was widespread, and as late as 1820,

10. Davis Diary, April 14, 15, and Miscellaneous 2, 1865.

most black Pennsylvanians in rural communities were indentured to whites.[11] Although we might hope that Isaac Davis and his wife made their way to Pennsylvania to ensure that their children were born into freedom, they might have also been "freed" into extended indenture, their own freedom still in limbo.

The last vestiges of slavery faded in Pennsylvania as the fugitive slave crisis heated up. By 1850, armed engagements broke out with some regularity, with free blacks and their sympathetic white neighbors defending themselves and their property from slave catchers and their proxies coming in from Maryland, Delaware, and Virginia. Angry with Pennsylvanians who refused to return suspected fugitives, Virginians and Marylanders demanded vengeance on the citizens of Pennsylvania for their recalcitrance. Well-known cases, such as the Christiana Riot in Lancaster County in 1851, have received a good deal of attention, but small skirmishes broke out all over south-central Pennsylvania.[12] The Davis family lived in Lancaster County some time around 1839, when Emilie was born, but by 1850, Isaac and his son, Alfred, were living in Pottsville, Schuylkill County. If they were aware of the riot in Christiana the next year, Isaac and Alfred likely were relieved to be removed from the fighting along the state's southern border. Even so, free blacks throughout Pennsylvania felt increasingly vulnerable to abduction and rendition to the South. Isaac's Maryland birth may have made him feel unsafe, except that his advanced age (Isaac was fifty years old in 1850) made him an unlikely candidate for rendition.

Because of its small but vocal abolitionist community, Philadelphia provided some measure of safety for fugitives like those involved in the Christiana riot. With a black population of 22,000 by midcentury, Philadelphia boasted the largest free black population of any northern city.[13] Martin Delany once described northern blacks as a "nation within a nation" because of the racism they continued to endure and the institutions they built to shield themselves from it.[14] At the center of Philadelphia's black community stood a group

---

11. Nash and Soderlund, *Freedom by Degrees*, 181–93.

12. Harrold, *Border War*, 150–57.

13. Weigley, "Border City," 385.

14. Martin Delany, quoted in Dubin and Biddle, *Tasting Freedom*, 102.

of prominent black families, including the Purvises, Fortens, and Whites, and the web of black churches, schools, benevolence organizations, and civil rights organizations they built. Linked by marriage and political activism, the families of Robert Purvis, James Forten, and Jacob White formed what historian Emma Lapsansky has called "a dynasty of social activists."[15] Robert Purvis, James McCrummel, and William Still led the Philadelphia Vigilance Committee, which served as the nerve center of the region's Underground Railroad; here, operatives gathered and disseminated intelligence intended to protect fugitive slaves from capture. Still helped hundreds of fugitives escape and did historians the favor of keeping track of their names, the circumstances surrounding their escape, and their destination when they left Philadelphia.[16]

When the Davises relocated to Philadelphia, they joined a vibrant black community eager to bring on a war over slavery and a white community that was openly hostile to them.[17] Black Philadelphians were excluded from concert halls, public transportation, schools, churches, meeting halls, and other public places, and they were harassed and assaulted in their own neighborhoods. Their churches and meeting places were attacked. White Philadelphians were virulently opposed to even the mildest expressions of antislavery positions. In 1859, the mayor of Philadelphia, Alexander Henry, would not allow Mary Brown, John Brown's widow, to stop in Philadelphia with her husband's remains for fear that a mob would attack the train.[18] And days before South Carolina's legislature drew up orders of secession in December 1860, city leaders called on Philadelphians to renew their commitment to *returning* fugitive slaves in order to reassure slaveholding states of their commitment to protecting

15. Lapsansky, "World the Agitators Made," 96.

16. Still, *Underground Railroad*. James A. McGowan transferred the names, dates, and other data from Still's account into an eminently searchable Excel spreadsheet called the McGowan Index, hosted by the Temple University Libraries at http://guides.temple.edu/content.php?pid=5056&sid=33737.

17. Emilie's brother, Elijah Davis (often called EJ in the diary), was living in Philadelphia by 1844 and worked as a waiter; see the list of people and institutions in the front matter of this volume. *McElroy's Philadelphia City Directory*, http://www.philageohistory.org/rdic -images/index2.cfm (accessed January 30, 2013).

18. DeCaro, *John Brown*, 96.

slavery.[19] Frederick Douglass believed that there was not a city to be found "in which prejudice against color is more rampant than in Philadelphia."[20]

Although there was nothing new about the sentiments of white Philadelphians, young black Philadelphians seemed more willing to confront prejudice directly. In March 1860, for example, a group of young activists tried to rescue a fugitive who had been ordered to return to slavery, attacking federal marshals as they led the man to the train station.[21] Although the rescue attempt failed, the bold attack on federal officials signaled a new militancy among activists one generation removed from the likes of William Still and Robert Purvis. Raised in politically active households and trained in elite black schools, men and women like Octavius Catto, Jacob White Jr., and the teacher Caroline LeCount came together in the classrooms of the Institute for Colored Youth. These were Emilie's teachers and fellow parishioners at her church—and her friends and confidantes.

Our first record of Emilie locates her at the home of her brother, Elijah Davis, in the Seventh Ward, a swath of today's Center City bound (north and south) by Spruce and South Streets, and (west and east) by the Schuylkill River and Seventh Street.[22] Her diary entries suggest that she remained in the Seventh Ward when she began living on her own. In 1897–98, W. E. B. Du Bois described the Seventh Ward—by then, a dense mix of Jews, Italians, and African Americans—as a "slum" for its "dirt, drunkenness, poverty and crime. Murder sat at our doorsteps, police were our government and philanthropy dropped in with periodic advice."[23] At midcentury, though, the neighborhood served as the center of black cultural and

19. "Union Meeting in Independence Square," *Public Ledger*, December 14, 1860, 1; "The Great Meeting, A Day for the Union," *Philadelphia Inquirer*, December 14, 1860, 1; "Speech of the Honorable Joseph R. Ingersoll," *Philadelphia Inquirer*, December 14, 1860, 2.

20. Frederick Douglass, quoted in Weigley, "Border City," 386.

21. Dubin and Biddle, *Tasting Freedom*, 241–44.

22. Like Isaac, Elijah was born in Maryland in 1820; he lived in the Seventh Ward between 1860 and 1862. 1860 United States Federal Census, Philadelphia Ward 7, Philadelphia, Pennsylvania, roll M653_1157, page 58, image 62, family history library film 805157; see also *McElroy's Philadelphia City Directory*, http://www.philageohistory.org/rdic-images/index2.cfm (accessed January 30, 2013).

23. Du Bois, *Autobiography*, 195.

FIGURE 3   Seventh Ward row houses on Pine Street, 1870. Emilie lived in the Seventh Ward, a neighborhood that offered easy access to school and church and to the homes of those for whom she sewed. Here, too, she frequently attended lectures, concerts, and meetings and visited with friends and family. The Library Company of Philadelphia. Photo: Alfred H. Hemple.

political life, and black ward residents were conveniently located within easy walking distance to the homes of the elite where many of them worked. Just across Spruce was the Eighth Ward, which extended north four blocks to Chestnut; the Fifth Ward was located immediately east of the Seventh and Eighth Wards, extending from Seventh Street to the Delaware River. Blacks lived in both wards in substantial numbers.[24] Though not yet a numerically significant proportion of the entire city population, Philadelphians of color lived and worked in the middle of the city and enjoyed the institutional support of three contiguous neighborhoods.

Within these neighborhoods, women of color were a strong presence. In 1860, 13,008 "free colored women" and 9,177 "free colored men" lived in Philadelphia County.[25] Du Bois found the same gender imbalance in 1890 and traced it back as far as 1820. He chalked up the "unusual excess of females" to their employment in domestic

24. Weigley, "Border City," 385–86.
25. County-level results for 1860, University of Virginia Library Historical Census Browser, http://mapserver.lib.virginia.edu/php/county.php.

service and to the limited work opportunities open to black men. To Du Bois, this "disproportion" indicated "an unhealthy condition," and he blamed it for the high rate of illegitimacy. Du Bois worried, too, that because lower-class men were often included in middle-class "social gatherings" as a way of correcting the gender imbalance, outsiders might get the "impression that the social level of the women is higher than the level of the men."[26]

Du Bois's concerns aside, Emilie Davis enjoyed strong bonds of friendship with the women in her life. Diary readers will note Emilie's frequent references to Nel (Nell, Nellie), Sue, Cristy, Mary, Hannah, Lizzie, Celestine, and Rachel, to name a few. These women provided Emilie with critical support and a sense of community while she was living on her own in the city. As historian Erica Dunbar has shown, even though they were denied leadership roles in the city's black churches, women played a critical role in enforcing acceptable behavior, sustaining the community's poorest members, and establishing schools for and teaching black youth.[27] As a domestic, Emilie would never be counted as part of the city's black elite, but by building strong bonds with women and men in her church, school, and voluntary work, she situated herself comfortably within the larger black community that grew up around the elite. Emilie visited her friends regularly, wrote to them when she could not, exchanged friendship albums, and kept a diary.[28] After she married, Emilie donated money to her church and rented a pew in her own name, indications that she continued to take an interest in the community even as her own domestic responsibilities began to mount.[29]

In the diary, Emilie practiced her penmanship, which was a critical part of her self-representation. Like careful attention to clothing and hair, good penmanship and correct spelling marked the author of a letter or of an entry in an album as a lady. While her diary was intended to be private, Emilie engaged in all sorts of semipublic

26. Du Bois, *Philadelphia Negro*, 53–55n5.

27. Dunbar, *Fragile Freedom*, 51–52, 58–69.

28. For more on friendship albums, see ibid., 122–25.

29. "Miss E. White," $25, Free-Will Offering, First African Presbyterian Church, December 30, 1877, American Negro Historical Society Collection, HSP.

activities—she sat for photographs, exchanged letters, and began a friendship album—that were intended to cement her friendships and to establish her respectability within her peer group. Writing in her diary helped Emilie keep track of the letters she sent and the visits she owed; in its pages, too, she offered her own judgments about the good and bad behavior of community members. When she occasionally weighed in on the immorality of others—as in 1863, when she writes that Georgiana's abusive husband "disgraced her shamfuly" when he beat her—we appreciate how much significance Emilie Davis and others in her community placed on respectable behavior.[30] To insulate themselves from white racism, black Philadelphians enforced strict behavioral standards, denied offenders the support of the community, and hid some infractions from white scrutiny.

Perhaps this reflexive privacy explains the frustrating lack of sources that historians of black Philadelphia face in writing their history. Although black Philadelphians participated in a thick network of institutions, few records remain to tell their stories. The meeting minutes and annual reports of organizations like the Philadelphia Female Anti-Slavery Society and the Ladies' Union Association offer researchers brief glimpses of the political and humanitarian relief work of women like Emilie Davis, but institutions that stood at the heart of black Philadelphia—Mother Bethel African Methodist Episcopal Church, for instance, and the Institute for Colored Youth—have few records that date to this period.[31] Mother Bethel's newspaper, the *Christian Recorder*, is a notable exception, and the paper is a vital primary source for uncovering the history of black Philadelphia. A surprising evidentiary silence surrounds Philadelphia's black elite, too, with few or no family papers for the Cattos, Fortens, and Purvises. To write their biography of Octavius Catto, Murray Dubin and Dan Biddle relied heavily on the *Christian Recorder*, the *Philadelphia Inquirer*, and other local dailies. Julie Winch overcame similar odds, finding James Forten's papers scattered in unlikely places

30. Davis Diary, Memoranda 4, 1863.
31. Like the PFASS records, the Ladies' Union Association (LUA) records are located at HSP.

and his newspaper articles often written under pen names.[32] In her biography of Robert Purvis, Margaret Hope Bacon compensated for the absence of family papers by relying on the papers of Purvis's extensive abolitionist connections.[33] They ran successful businesses, sent their children to school and tutored them at home, created and sustained societies, and lobbied for civil rights, but either they left no papers or these papers have not yet been identified. Mystery surrounds the recent discovery of Emilie Davis's diaries, which were purchased by the Historical Society of Pennsylvania in 1999. Perhaps there are other such sources in personal collections that will allow us to build outward for a more complete picture of the wartime city.

Until then, Emilie Davis's diaries open a small and very personal window onto this vibrant black community. Emilie comments on the Civil War's moments of elation and despair and, more than anything, its daily gnawing uncertainty. We hope readers will allow themselves to forget what they think they know about the war and to *live* its memorable days, with Emilie Davis's pen as their guide.

32. Winch, *Gentleman of Color*, 7.   33. Bacon, *But One Race*, ix.

FIGURE 4   Plan of Philadelphia, 1860. More than twenty thousand African Americans lived in neighborhoods throughout Philadelphia at midcentury. Black Philadelphians often made their homes, built churches, and opened schools in a swath of today's Center City, including the Seventh, Eighth, and Fifth Wards. Plan of Philadelphia (DAMS 3906), Of 610 1860 M, Historical Society of Pennsylvania. Inset and labels by David Uspal and Joanne Quinn, Villanova University.

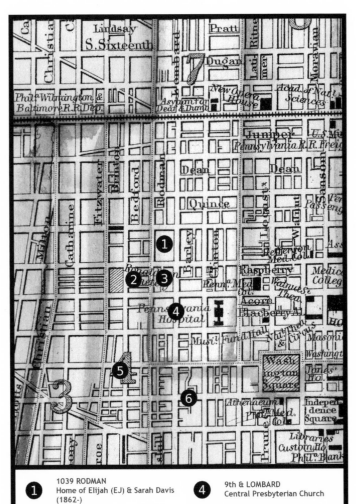

1 1039 RODMAN
Home of Elijah (EJ) & Sarah Davis
(1862-)

2 900 BAINBRIDGE
Institute for Colored Youth
(School)

3 910 RODMAN
Home of Elijah (EJ) & Sarah Davis
(1860-1861)

4 9th & LOMBARD
Central Presbyterian Church

5 7th STREET BELOW SHIPPEN
7th St. Presbyterian Church

6 419 S. 6th STREET
Mother Bethel African Methodist
Episcopal Church

1863

THURSDAY, JANUARY 1, 1863.

To day has bin a memorable day[1] and i thank god i have bin sperd to see it the day was religously observed all the churches were open we had quite a Jubiliee in the evenin i went to Joness to a Party had a very pleasent time

FRIDAY 2

Beutiful day[2] Nellie[3] was up and spent Part of the day reading[4] was here Nellie had an engagement and had to go home i stoped home a few minutes the girls were

1. The Emancipation Proclamation became official on January 1, 1863. Philadelphia's black community celebrated emancipation by crowding into the city's black churches minutes before the New Year; at midnight, Philadelphians of color cheered the president's proclamation. Dubin and Biddle, *Tasting Freedom*, 277–78; "Meetings and Demonstrations," *Christian Recorder* (Philadelphia), January 10, 1863.

2. Like most diarists, Emilie regularly reports on the weather. Rain, snow, or extreme temperatures at times prevented her daily travels, as she walked to work, school, and church.

3. Nellie (also called Nell or Nel) appears often in the diary. It is unclear to whom Emilie was referring, but Nellie may have been Caroline E. White, the wife of Jacob C. White Jr. See the diary entry for February 20, 1863, and the list of people and institutions in the front matter of this volume.

4. Emilie refers to a "reading" and "redding" in other entries; this is likely the same person.

SATURDAY 3

all there very Pleasant this morning buisey all day reading and his
were her [here] to service i went down home[5] to see if father[6] had
begun and was coming away when

SUNDAY, JANUARY 4, 1863.

he cam i was delighted to see him i did not go to church in the
morning very good Discours in the afternoon Dave was down we had
a full choir bible class at gertrudes very interresting

MONDAY 5

quite Pleasant to day Nellie was up a little while reading went away
this morning singing school begins tonight[7] we all went down several
strangers were there i was quite mortified to see so few

TUESDAY 6

out we did not do any business very dull to day raining in the
afternoon i went down home heard som good news Tom is here
i went to meeting[8] very

---

5. In 1860, Emilie Davis was twenty-one years old and living in the home of her uncle, Elijah Davis. (Emilie's occupation is listed as "servant" in the census, suggesting that her frequent references to sewing in the diary were related to her work as a domestic servant.) Also resident in the home were Elijah's wife, Sarah, and the couple's son, Elwood; Elizabeth Davis; and Thomas Davis (see the list of people and institutions in the front matter of this volume). By 1863, Emilie appears to be living on her own. At times, she lives with employers on the outskirts of Philadelphia. 1860 United States Federal Census, Philadelphia Ward 7, Philadelphia, Pennsylvania, roll M653_1157, page 58, image 62, family history library film 805157.

6. Census records suggest that Emilie Davis's father is Isaac Davis (see the list of people and institutions in the front matter of this volume). 1860 United

States Federal Census, Harrisburg Ward 4, Dauphin, Pennsylvania, roll M653_1104, page 1104, image 501, family history library film 805104.

7. Emilie attended the Institute for Colored Youth (ICY), a coeducational Quaker school opened in 1837 and located on the 900 block of Bainbridge Street (see the list of people and institutions in the front matter of this volume). The students, including Emilie and many of her friends mentioned in the diary, attended school every Monday evening until May 25, 1863. Conyers, *A Living Legend*, 16–23; "Annual Report of the Managers of the Institute for Colored Youth," *Christian Recorder*, October 8, 1864.

8. On Tuesdays, church members—including the Bustills, Whites, Gibbs, and Browns—held meetings at their homes. Emilie regretted those rare occasions when she had to miss Tuesday meeting.

May 1859

Photograph.   By Richards.

St Thomas' (African) Church.
Southwest corner of High and Adelphi street. (Episcopal.)

FIGURE 5   St. Thomas (African) Protestant Episcopal Church, 1859. Although Emilie's regular church was Seventh Street Presbyterian Church, she also attended events at St. Thomas, located at Adelphi and Fifth Streets, between Locust and Walnut. The Library Company of Philadelphia. Photo: Frederick DeBourg Richards.

WEDNESDAY, JANUARY 7, 1863.

few out but we had a good meeting the girls called to see me to day
i saw alfred[9] last night he did not say he sent me the album[10] but i
know he did Nell and Sue were up here tonight

THURSDAY 8

very stormy to day did not go any were but home and Marys liz and
stephen at Mr Joneses Nellie bought the long talked of gloves for
Cristy i spent the evening home with father

FRIDAY 9

very dull i had a letter from lile to day liz Williams brought it up
Vincent[11] was up here this evening he brought me a

SATURDAY, JANUARY 10, 1863.

a hansome album from a Phelopeno Present i am delighted with it
it rained so i did not go out i was very buisy with my dres i cut the
body out

SUNDAY 11

very Pleasent most too much so for the time of year I went to church
in the morning mr. gibbs[12] was not there mr guy[13] spoke his remarkes
were very good after church we went

9. Alfred, Emilie's brother, was thirty years old in 1863; he lived in Pottsville, Pennsylvania, until 1860 (see the list of people and institutions in the front matter of this volume). 1850 United States Federal Census, Pottsville South Ward, Schuylkill, Pennsylvania, roll M432_827, page 376A, image 690; 1860 United States Federal Census, Pottsville North West Ward, Schuylkill, Pennsylvania, roll M653_1178, page 479, image 484, family history library film 805178.

10. In the nineteenth century, women often kept friendship albums, small books passed among friends to record prose, poetry, thoughts, well wishes, and signatures. These albums often included small photographs of friends, family members, or public figures. For African American women, friendship albums were a means of maintaining important relationships

and networks among women who only saw each other at political and social events. Dunbar, *Fragile Freedom*, 122–28.

11. Emilie's relationship with Vincent is unspecified in the diary, but it appears that they are romantically involved during this period of Emilie's life.

12. Emilie attended the Seventh Street Presbyterian Church, alternatively called the First (Colored) Presbyterian Church, located on Seventh Street, below Shippen (currently Bainbridge Street). Jonathan C. Gibbs was pastor of the church; see the list of people and institutions in the front matter of this volume. Services were offered every morning at 10 o'clock and in the afternoon at 3 o'clock. "Church Directory," *Christian Recorder*, January 17, 1863.

13. Mr. Alexander Guy, sixty-nine years old, was an officer in the proceedings

MONDAY 12

to see Nellies grandma Father spent this day with alfred I spent the
afternoon and evening in reading and singing no one cam

TUESDAY, JANUARY 13, 1863.

up to see me i went down to school last night we had a very nice
school we elected officers for this year Dave was down Nellie stoped
to go to meeting Mary J and her son were

WEDNESDAY 14

here how glad i was to see them he is a fine boy Nellie was up here
this afternoon she is afraid to com up at night

THURSDAY 15

Mary and i went out shoping Mary Simson was married this morning
at 8 o clock Stoped at our hous for dinner then when home to
Bridesburg Mary Crasis was bridesmaid[14]

FRIDAY, JANUARY 16, 1863.

[strikethrough] last night i spent a very agreeable evening at agustes
with Nellie Cristy and Mary very favorite Nellie did not get up here
to day i have not bin out all

SATURDAY 17

day very stormy[15] yesterday morning in the afternoon father whent
out to Mr Cales Sue was up here this evening very cold i stoped down
home and at Nell she was quite scick

to permit Rev. Gibbs to leave the Seventh
Street Presbyterian Church on good terms
for future endeavors, according to the
Recorder. A later notice indicates that Emi-
lie and EJ each donated one dollar to the
Committee of the Banneker Institute to
the "[f]und for the purpose of circulating
speeches and documents favorable to uni-
versal suffrage." "Notices and Local Items.
Tribute of Respect for Rev. Jonathan C.
Gibbs," *Christian Recorder*, March 17, 1866;
"Banneker Institute," *Christian Recorder*,
April 19, 1866; 1870 United States Federal
Census, Philadelphia Ward 8 Dist 22 (2nd
Enum), Philadelphia, Pennsylvania, roll
M593_1421, page 305A, image 613, family
history library film 552920.

14.   The *Recorder* carried Mary Simpson's marriage announcement: "[o]n the
15th, Mr. Gideon H. Pierce, of Bridgeton,
New Jersey, and Miss Mary Cornelia
Simpson, of Princeton, N.J[.]" were
married." "Married," *Christian Recorder*,
January 31, 1863.

15.   The *Inquirer* noted that the rain
had caused the river to rise in Louisville,

SUNDAY 18

clear and cold this morning i did not go to church in the morning
in the afternoon i went out with father to cales we had a missionary
to Preach for us

MONDAY, JANUARY 19, 1863.

in the afternoon in the evening we had a very nice Bible class great
many out I wrote two letters yester morning quite cold sue and Nellie
were up here i went down to school we had

TUESDAY 20

no teacer but will have one next monday night vincent came home
with me I was down there this morning father was well i went to
meeting we had a very nice mee

WEDNESDAY 21

ting [meeting] lizzie brown was up here yesterday very stormy all day
bin in the house all day Nellie did not get up here this evening

THURSDAY, JANUARY 22, 1863.

very dull Nellie and i went out shoping she bought a dress and i cut it
out for her lizzie stoped at our house and staid untill it was time to go
to the lecture[16] we went to the

FRIDAY 23

lecture it was very good not many out owing to the weather very
Pleasent to day I stoped at Meals this morning her hand was better
Nellie was up and spent the evening Cristy was up

Pennsylvania. This was most likely a
reference to the Delaware River, which
runs between Philadelphia and Camden,
New Jersey. Had the Delaware risen in
Louisville, the high water would have
flowed south into the city. "The Weather,"
Philadelphia Inquirer, January 19, 1863.

16. Emilie frequently attended
lectures, though in her diary she rarely
provided identifying details. The First

(Colored) Presbyterian Church hosted
weekly lectures on Friday nights at
7 o'clock at the Benezet Hall, on Seventh
Street, below Lombard Street. The Central
Presbyterian Church at Ninth and Lombard Streets, approximately two blocks
from Emilie's church, hosted weekly
lectures on Thursday nights at 8 o'clock.
"Church Directory," *Christian Recorder*,
January 17, 1863.

SATURDAY 24

she was not well very cloudy today Sue was up her this evening went
down town had quite a Pleasent chat with Father stoped at Nells a
little while she was buisy finishing her Dress

SUNDAY, JANUARY 25, 1863.

cloudy in the morning clear in the afternoon we had an excelent
sermon this morning mr gibbs was very impressive I went down to
hear the children Practice in the afternoon Mary was up to

MONDAY 26

see me in the evening Sue an Mr Cooper called very dull morning
lizzie cam up and spent the afternoon with me and staid to tea
we went down to school together

TUESDAY 27

Nellie was here a little while very Poor school no teacher Dave
DeClones teaching us again meeting at Fabauxs we had a happy time
it was good to be there

WEDNESDAY, JANUARY 28, 1863.

Poor Tomy[17] had to go to the gard house yesterday he did not want go
very heavy storm today snowing all day and night Nellie has no [. . .]

THURSDAY 29

Storming a little sue spent the morning with me I spent a very
agreeable time at home to day Dave was maried to night [tonight]
and I had to march

FRIDAY 30

in Jon Gorge and Jake[18] were at the wedding Lizzie was here to day
Poor girl i feel sorry for her

17. Thomas Davis enlisted in the
U.S. Navy in 1862, when he was fourteen
years old (see the list of people and
institutions in the front matter of this
volume). This reference to the guardhouse
suggests that the young seaman was being
punished for a behavioral infraction.

National Park Service, Civil War Service
Records, http://www.nps.gov/civilwar/
search-sailors-detail.htm?sailors_id=
Davo178.

18. This is likely a reference to George
Bustill White and his brother, Jacob
(Jake) White Jr. (see the list of people and

FIGURE 6 Jacob C. White Jr. Along with his brother George Bustill White, Jacob C. White Jr. attended the Institute for Colored Youth. He became the principal of the Roberts Vaux Primary School in 1864. Charles L. Blockson Afro-American Collection, Temple University Libraries.

SATURDAY, JANUARY 31, 1863.

Sue stoped here to night and we went out together she goes to
Wisters on monday i went in home had quite a Pleasent visit stoped
in to see Nellie she

SUNDAY, FEBRUARY 1

Was rather dry rather cloudy to day i did not go to church in the
morning In the afternoon we had an excelent sermon Bible class
at class very rainy gorge and i called

MONDAY 2

on the bride Nellie treated me very shaby yesterday with out a cause
we had a very interesting class very fine day i had a letter from Johns
i went down town to school it was quite encouraging

TUESDAY, FEBRUARY 3, 1863.

we had to open school ourselves meeting at holmes very few out very
cold and no fire Nellies home and could not go Mr frebeux lead the
meeting

WEDNESDAY 4

bitter cold day i have not ventured out to day Nellie being lame she
wont get up here i have bin very buisy sewing all this evening

THURSDAY 5

very cold Mary was up here this morning she went to [. . .] I went
home and did not get mush [much] better in the evening i went to
virgil lecture

FRIDAY, FEBRUARY 6, 1863.

he lectured well very few there owing to the weather it very
unfaverable it was raining very fast [strikethrough] when i came
home egerton cam home with me I was home a few minute

---

institutions in the front matter of this
volume). Jacob was elected president of
the Banneker Institute in 1863 and was
"[t]he catalyst and hub of the organization," according to historian Emma
Jones Lapsansky. "Banneker Institute of
Philadelphia," *Christian Recorder*, January 24, 1863; Lapsansky, "'Discipline to the
Mind,'" 86–87.

SATURDAY 7

this afternoon it is a beutiful day as warm as it was Colie Sarah Mary and i went down to see Tomy this afternoon we found him well but ansious

SUNDAY 8

to get off very fine day i went to church this morning herd a good sermon i spent the afternoon in reading mrs bunt and sue stoped to see me Nellie has not bin

MONDAY, FEBRUARY 9, 1863.

up here for some time on a Sunday evening very fine day Nellie was up this afternoon an staid untill i went to school no teacher yet or any Prospects

TUESDAY 10

of any John an Sue has make up again i have bin sick[19] all day did not go to meeting Poor lizzie is sick Nellie was here i wrote to read

WEDNESDAY 11

ing [Reading] very Pleasent this morning Mary was up to see me Father is not well Nell and Sue stoped it has bin snowing

THURSDAY, FEBRUARY 12, 1863.

very dull day raining all the time i was out i did not go any Place but home and in Nellies i spent the Best Part of the evening with father i feel so glad i have the opportunity

FRIDAY 13

of spending an evening with him egerton came home with me last night sue and John have becom reconciled to each other Sue was here and spent the evening we had quite a nice

---

19. The regularity of Emilie's references to being sick or feeling ill suggests that the diarist might be referring to her menstrual cycle. Historian Joan Jacobs Brumberg, in her extensive study of girls' diaries, found that "some Victorian adolescents made brief comments in their diaries to being 'unwell' . . . every twenty-eight to thirty days," though "most said nothing at all." Brumberg, *Body Project*, xxvii.

SATURDAY 14

time it is a lovely day to day it Valintines day and nellies birth day
how i would like to make her a present but i am not able at Present

SUNDAY, FEBRUARY 15, 1863.

very dull day i went to church in the afternoon we had quite a
milatary sermon after church we went to see Barker and aunt Jane[20]
she is quite sick Bible class at nellies it

MONDAY 16

was very nice but we did not read enough and let out too soon very
beutiful day we had no school st tomas concert[21] cam off tonight i did
not go Nellie bake din

TUESDAY 17

ner [dinner] with me yesterday quite a remarkable occourence
meeting at mrs riners very stormy showering all day very few were
there in consequence

WEDNESDAY, FEBRUARY 18, 1863.

it is very unpleasent to day it is my birthday nevertheless i feel
thankful i have bin spard so long and if i should be spard in future
i will try and spend my

20. Aunt Jane appears to be Isaac's sister and Emilie's aunt (see the list of people and institutions in the front matter of this volume). Two women named Jane Davis, identified in the 1860 census, are likely prospects. 1860 United States Federal Census, Philadelphia Ward 14 Division 2, Philadelphia, Pennsylvania, roll M653_1164, page 513, image 519, family history library film 805164; Philadelphia Ward 5 Southern Division, Philadelphia, Pennsylvania, roll M653_1155, page 536, image 542, family history library film 805155.

21. Church choirs organized and held fundraising concerts. According to the *Recorder*, the concert Emilie mentions here attracted a large crowd, as "many could not gain admittance." The entertainment included "singing, and solos, assisted by a melodeon, flute, bass violene, and . . . a fiddle." St. Thomas (African) Protestant Episcopal Church was located at Fifth and Adelphi Streets, between Locust and Walnut. "Exhibition at St. Thomas' Church on Last Monday Night," *Christian Recorder*, February 21, 1863; Catto, *A Semi-Centenary Discourse*, 107.

THURSDAY 19

time more Profitable very unpleasent day Nellie and i went out shoping muslins are frightfuly Dear in the evening we went to the lecture after witch we over to rachels then up to

FRIDAY 20

nellies Jake mad nellie birthday Presents very dull day we expected Tomy but he didnot com this afternoon i went up to see Celistene[22] she is

SATURDAY, FEBRUARY 21, 1863.

much better clear and cold today Nellie was up this morning i went down to rachels saw Cristiee and sally Sue was down waiting for me when i got home

SUNDAY 22

Father was not well yesterday very stormy[23] i have not bin able to go to church all day it snowed all day sue cald here this evening throught [through] all the snow

MONDAY 23

very fine day sue and i went out shoping stoped to see Celly in the evening we went down to school it was very cherles

TUESDAY, FEBRUARY 24, 1863.

liz was not down Cristy tried to Put on french sue cam down about 10 Mr Haas died yesterday morning i did not go to meeting spent

WEDNESDAY 25

Part of the evening with father fine day nellie has not bin here to day they had pratising for the funeral this evening i did not go Sue and John stoped as they went home

22. This may be Celestine Clark, listed as an eighteen-year-old "mulatto" living in the First Ward in the 1870 census, but this would have made her only eleven years old when Emilie mentioned her in the diary. 1870 United States Federal Census, Philadelphia Ward 1 District 3, Philadelphia, Pennsylvania, roll M593_1387, page 576A, image 471, family history library film 552886.

23. On this date, a significant snowstorm affected much of the northeast. The *Inquirer* reported that it was snowing in Baltimore, New York City, and Buffalo, New York. "The Snow Storm," *Philadelphia Inquirer*, February 23, 1863.

THURSDAY 26

Very wet day i went down to the church very large furneal [funeral]
considering the wet day Mr Cato[24] was there Mr gibbs spoke butiful
Dear old man he lived

FRIDAY, FEBRUARY 27, 1863.

A Cristian linfe and he died like a Cristian oh that i may be calm in
my last moments and Prepared sue spent the evening with me how i
will miss her when she

SATURDAY 28

goes to germantown very fine day mary gertrude and i went down
to see tomy and had quite a Pleasent visit he is very ansious to com a
home

SUNDAY, MARCH 1

raining in the morning I went to church this af ternoon it was
crowded an it was a very solemn servis bible class was at mrs. riders
we had quite

MONDAY, MARCH 2, 1863.

a nice class lovely day Nellie and Sue were here mary and her friend
Sue went out to germantown today i went down to school tonight
no teacher yet the fair comences tonight

TUESDAY 3[25]

John simson came home with me last night meeting out to Clayes
very few out quite a cold meeting after meeting i went to nellies
coming up home i met John he came

---

24. William Catto, father of Octavius V. Catto, was a minister at First African Presbyterian Church and a founding
member of the Banneker Institute. Emma
Jones Lapsansky writes that Rev. Catto
was "long a champion of education and
literacy" in Philadelphia and authored
a history of the city's black churches.
Lapsansky, "'Discipline to the Mind,'"
86–87.

25. On March 3, 1863, the U.S. gov-
ernment issued the National Enrollment
Act as a form of conscription. However,
African Americans in Pennsylvania
were not permitted to enlist in their
state until mid-1863. In the meantime,
Pennsylvanians of color traveled north to
enlist in the Massachusetts 54th or 55th
Regiments. Binder, "Pennsylvania Negro
Regiments," 383–417.

WEDNESDAY 4

up with me beutiful day but quite marshy Nellie did not com up as usal i stoped to see lizzie brown John is quite sick

THURSDAY, MARCH 5, 1863.

The first clear Thursday we have had for som time sue was in this morning i Paid a visit to Joneses to day Nellie we stoped at aunt Janes then went to the lecture after

FRIDAY 6

The wich i went to the fair Dave cam home with me lamind stoped to Sue sent for John to com out I Droped a note to Cristy to tell him

SATURDAY 7

very stormy Nellie stoped here she was very wet Tomy got leave of absense to he has to report on Monday

SUNDAY, MARCH 8, 1863.

very rainy day i went to Church in the mor'ng mr gibbs was sick consequncely mr white held forth very few out neither of the girls were out there cousin died this morning

MONDAY 9

Tomy came up and spent the afternoon i spent a very lonsome evening very fine day Nellie wes up she did not go down to school cristy and i went over about half past 8 no one

TUESDAY 10

came down but gorge after school gorge and i went to the fair he was very gallant showing meeting up at whites i fear few were there

WEDNESDAY, MARCH 11, 1863.

it being so stormy hannah brown stoped to see me to day my side has bin very troubelsom every since mondy the huctchinsons give a concert[26] to

---

26. The Hutchinson Family gave a benefit concert for the "S.C. Statistical Association of the Colored People of Pennsylvania" at Sansom Street Hall. The group sang songs about "home, patriotism, and freedom." Tickets cost twenty-five cents. For more on the association, see the list of people and institutions in the front

THURSDAY 12

night to is one of [. . .] hes one day as one minut it is clear the next it is snowing Nellie and i went to have our Photagraphhes taken but we did not succede we went

FRIDAY 13

to see Celestine I was quite sick all the evening Nellie and i stood for our Photagrapphe[27] this afternoon

SATURDAY, MARCH 14, 1863.

clear to day i went up to lizzie White spent quite a Pleasent time with her she is very Deaf went down home to see father satdy

SUNDAY 15

very cold very fine morning snow in the afternoon we had an excellent sermon this afternoon Dr. Jones Preach mr gibbs is still sick we have quite a nice class

MONDAY 16

notwithstanding the storm all the young were there but Vincent no school to night we have Decided not to go down untile we have a teacher Nellie and I went up to lizzie

TUESDAY, MARCH 17, 1863.

last evening Vincent looked perfectly [. . .] we went in Fred Duglass lectures[28] to night meeting at Stills mr gibbs was down in the room but did not

---

matter of this volume. "The Hutchinson Family, 'Tribe of Asa,'" *Christian Recorder*, March 7, 1863; Weigley, "Border City," 415–16.

27. Advertisements for establishments such as the "Photograph Gallery of Mr. B. F. Reimer" and "Mr. Brown" encouraged Philadelphians to have their photos taken. Reimer's galleries were located at 615 and 617 North Second Street and No. 624 Arch Street. Reimer's advertisement promised that the photographers made "no distinction as to color,

or between rich and poor, but [treated] all with the same graceful and natural consideration." Mr. Brown was located on Sixth Street, above Walnut. "Photographs," *Christian Recorder*, April 18, 1863; "Photographs," *Christian Recorder*, May 12, 1864. For more information about the significance of African Americans' access to photography, see Gallman, "Snapshots," 127–51.

28. Frederick Douglass, "the great hero and unfaltering Anglo-Saxon African opponent of slavery," lectured at the

WEDNESDAY 18

take any part in the meeting barker cam up for Nellie the hutchinsons give a concert[29] next Thurs day night for the benifit of our church i am quite disappointed

THURSDAY 19

nell did not com up i went up to hannahs then over to see aunt lizzy first sold 3 ticets[30] Sue was in town to day cam to the concert no lecture this i hardly no what

FRIDAY, MARCH 20, 1863.

to do with myself had to march Sarah Thomas and Mr Shim and fairy were at Nellies yesterday Shim is fine looking Nellie cam up this afternoon and we had one

SATURDAY 21

of oure old time talks

SUNDAY 22

very fine day i went to Church in the morning with neal mr gibbs is still sick Mr farhaux[31] exsorted for us i went down to hear the children Practice very lonsome in the evening

---

ICY to a full house. The *Recorder* did not mention the subject of the lecture, though Douglass evidently spoke on "common sense" matters. "Lectures by Frederick Douglass," *Christian Recorder*, March 21, 1863.

29.   Another concert by the Hutchinson Family, scheduled for March 26, was to benefit Emilie's church. The cost of a ticket was 25 cents for adults, 15 cents for children. "Singing," *Christian Recorder*, March 21, 1863.

30.   Emilie likely sold tickets for the Hutchinsons' March 26 concert.

31.   This may be a reference to a "Mr. J. C. Farbeaux," mentioned later in the *Recorder*. The 1870 census lists two men named Jacob Farbeaux residing in Philadelphia's Eighth Ward, both "colored" barbers; one was sixty-nine years old, and the other, thirty-eight. The Mr. Farbeaux mentioned in the diary was likely the former, as the *Recorder* notes that he chaired a church committee. "Notices and Local Items: Tribute of Respect for Rev. Jonathan C. Gibbs," *Christian Recorder*, March 17, 1866; 1870 United States Federal Census, Philadelphia Ward 8 District 22, Philadelphia, Pennsylvania, roll M593_1393, page 26A, image 55, family history library film 552892.

MONDAY, MARCH 23, 1863.

no one cam up to see me very fine day I was up to see Celestine and hannah Cely is quite sick again in Nellie and i went down to school we had a very nice school

TUESDAY 24

meeting at mr Decriss i did not go very stormy Nellie or liz was not there lizzie was here yesterday but i did not see her

WEDNESDAY 25

very fine day i have been very buisy trying to sell tickets for the concert Alfred bought one Nellie cam up this evening we had nice time

THURSDAY, MARCH 26, 1863.

very stormy to day i sold all my tickets Nell and rachel and went to the concert it was good every one seemed Pleased barker cam home

FRIDAY 27

with me and Vincent with rachel and Ellen I felt quite Displeased with Vincent i have not seen Nellie to day mary[32] Alfred is here in Mrs Clintons plase

SATURDAY 28

she went to the concert sarah and neal did not go neal expeccted to go to New York this morning i went down to see her off

SUNDAY, MARCH 29, 1863.

but she had a letter that liz was very sick she did not go very fine day mr gibbs still sick mr cuwar Preached this afternoon bible class was Postponed account of Confirmation

MONDAY 30

Nellie and went it was a Perfect fair Sue was in Cristy galanted us to Church but we had to march home Nellie was furious i went down to school we were down there

32. This is likely Alfred's wife, Mary.

TUESDAY 31

untill nine o clock before any one came Christy came down Nell run off from him meeting at bruces quite a nice meeting mrs hill lead liz was not [. . .]

WEDNESDAY, APRIL 1, 1863.

very fine day fer [for] the first i sent a letter to sister on mondy I have not bin out to day very buisey sewing father[33] talkes of going home next weeke Nell and Alfred were up we had a

THURSDAY 2

Jolly time quite stormy Em mccee paid me quite a long visit i went up to see mr gibbs he is better spent the evening home with father had to march as usal althou Crutices came home with me

FRIDAY 3

quite a Spring day i was out Promanading stoped at rachels Nellie and anna was up here this morning neal exppects to get off tomorrow

SATURDAY, APRIL 4, 1863.

quite a large fire near us last night neal leaft at 6 this morning Tomy sailed on Thursday for Port Roal [Royal][34] very stormy today snowing and hailing furiously

SUNDAY 5

very disagreeable day raining all the morning Nellie is not well i went down to Church Mr Cato Preached very fervant i spent quite a pleasent evening no one came

MONDAY 6

up to see me i spent the evening in reading the history of Abraham very dul day Nellie came up i went out 10 st and arch with her Mr gardeners

33. Emilie's father lived in Harrisburg; he had been visiting Philadelphia since the beginning of the year.

34. Tommy's ship, the USS *Cimarron*, served in the U.S. naval blockade off the coast of South Carolina—explaining

Emilie's reference to Port Royal, South Carolina. National Park Service, "Civil War Soldiers and Sailors System," http://www .nps.gov/civilwar/search-sailors-detail .htm?sailors_id=Davo178.

U. S. STEAMER CIMARRON.
off Charleston.

FIGURE 7 *USS Cimarron.* Thomas Davis served on a navy steamer, the USS *Cimarron*, pictured here as part of the blockade off the coast of Charleston, South Carolina. Unlike the army, the U.S. Navy never barred black men from service. When the Civil War began, several hundred black men were already in service. Naval History and Heritage Command, Washington, D.C., NH 61486.

TUESDAY, APRIL 7, 1863.

[Mr. Gardiner's] death[35] was announced yesterday although we expected it it was quite a shock we had no school last night we spent the evening at rachels the boyes are very carless about school

WEDNESDAY 8

Mr gardners body was rested in the church as was his request Nellie came up and spent the evening we had quite a nice time to our selves mary alfred is still

THURSDAY 9

at our house beutiful day i went down to the furneal mr gardener looked very badly he was so much swollen he had quite a holy furnal

FRIDAY, APRIL 10, 1863.

Mr Catto Preached his furneal sermon he spoke beutiful mr gibbs was not able to be there i know he regreted it Nellie spent the evening with me

SATURDAY 11

very fine day reading is in town he was here this morning and did Paid one of his sosiable visits i has bine quite sick all day stoped in home to father

SUNDAY 12

lovely morning i was not out in the afternoon the intercommunion was at st marys the servises werr very impressive bible class at stills i

MONDAY, APRIL 13, 1863.

did not go I was quite sick Monday not well i did not go out Nell was here for me to go down to school school is very poorly attended

35. Charles C. Gardiner, the pastor of another black Presbyterian church in Philadelphia and a teacher at the ICY, died from "dropsy" on April 6 in Harrisburg at the age of eighty-four. William Catto delivered the sermon at Gardiner's funeral. The *Recorder* described Gardiner as "one of the oldest Presbyterian ministers in this State. He was beloved by all who knew him. He was a friend to all sects and denominations." "Died," *Christian Recorder*, April 11, 1863.

TUESDAY 14

meeting at mrs hill father [. . .] of goin home Saturday we had a very good meeting father guy was so happy Nellie went to the lecture

WEDNESDAY 15

Stormy day little Frank[36] is quite sick mary is still here Nellie did not com up as.

THURSDAY, APRIL 16, 1863.

very dull day i was Down to Nell this morning we went out shopping she bout a dress and i ditto egerton was up to see me he did

FRIDAY 17

not go in to Nell I was supprised he is quite friendly i did no tell her he was in our house father was quite sick last night he is better today

SATURDAY 18

ran down to see father he is much better Nellie was up here this morning Johns was up to the house i did not see him

SUNDAY, APRIL 19, 1863.

very pleasant morning to day should be keep holy by every one i fear i do not observe it as much as i should mr gibbs spok for us it was like music to my ears to hear his voice

MONDAY 20

again rachel and lizzie spent the evening Christy cam for there we had quite a Pleasent talk no school to night raining quite hard Nell was up here part of the evening gorge is sick

TUESDAY 21

very Pleasant morning Father is talking about going home tomorrow how i shall miss him meeting in seventh st sullen i am ashamed to say i did not enjoy the

---

36. Frank is Mary and Alfred's son. Frank's illness might have delayed Mary's return home. Frank was seven years old in 1863, having been listed with his parents in the 1860 census at age four. 1860 United States Federal Census, Pottsville North West Ward, Schuylkill, Pennsylvania, roll M653_1178, page 479, image 484, family history library film 805178.

WEDNESDAY, APRIL 22, 1863.

meeting mr fabau and mr guy seemed so happy Father went home this morning i went up to the Depot[37] to see him off i felt so badly to see him go

THURSDAY 23

very disagreeable day mary nellie and i all went out shopping we meet reading he went along I spent part of the evening at marys and the other

FRIDAY 24

with Nell reading cam to bid me good by he had gone back to colleg sue was in to day it rained all the evening fred

SATURDAY, APRIL 25, 1863.

[Fred] Duglass[38] lectured last night at national hall stoped at nells to night and [. . .] we went around to marys barker Promised me his Photograph[39]

SUNDAY 26

very fine day very windy I went to church in the afternoon mr gibbs gave us a very good sermon Bible class at mrs hills very well attended

MONDAY 27

very grey did not get the we did not go down to school the boyes went down they did not like it he cursed we will not com down

37. Isaac Davis likely traveled in the smoking car of the train bound for Harrisburg, as train travel was segregated in Pennsylvania until integrated travel became law in the state in 1867. P. Foner, "Battle to End Discrimination (Part I)," 261–92, and P. Foner, "Battle to End Discrimination (Part II)," 368–72.

38. Frederick Douglass lectured on "The Affairs of the Nation" at National Hall on April 24. Sponsored by the ICY, Douglass's lecture occasioned two advertisements in the *Recorder*, one of which read, "[t]his is a worthy cause, and every colored lady and gentleman should lay by twenty-five cents, get a ticket, and go to the lecture." "The Alumni Association," *Christian Recorder*, April 11, 1863; "National Hall–National Hall. Frederick Douglass," *Christian Recorder*, April 11, 1863.

39. In the 1860s, photography became more accessible with the invention of *cartes-de-visite*, small photographs (about 3¼ by 2¼ inches) that could be produced inexpensively. Americans, both black and white, visited a photographer for the first time and exchanged photographs. Painter, *Sojourner Truth*, 185–86. See also Frederick Douglass, "Pictures and Progress," 1863, Howard University Archives, http://www.huarchivesnet.howard.edu/0002huarnet/freddoug.htm.

TUESDAY, APRIL 28, 1863.

very Pleasant meeting at rachels Nell was here last night we went around
to aunt Janes before meeting cristy came in [. . .] were barker had steped

WEDNESDAY 29

out very rainy all day I have bin very buisy with my Dress Nellie did
not com up glasters levee cam off to night Next sundy the long looked
for meeting comes off

THURSDAY 30

i finished wrighting William to day another stormy day to day is set
apart as a national fast day[40] i spent the evening home no letter

FRIDAY, MAY 1, 1863.

from father yet lovely day very warm Nell cam up this afternoon and
brought her sewing we spent the evening with [. . .] stoped here on
her way to

SATURDAY 2

the cars another lovely day how i would like to go [. . .] hannah
brown stoped here to night to see what i had to say about mr gibbs
i had nothing

SUNDAY 3

to say very fine day for the Weding mr gibbs Preached this morning
in the afternoon Docter [. . .] Delivered a beutiful Discours after the
sermon the

MONDAY, MAY 4, 1863.

Bridal parties came in and were married i expected to hear some
objection [. . .] not a word the bride looked lovely the church was
crowed no school Nell was up

40. The *Inquirer* reported that April 30
was a "day appointed by the President
of the United States for humiliation,
fasting, and prayer." Services were held
at various churches throughout the city,
all public and private offices were closed,
and public school children were granted
a vacation. Both Presidents Lincoln and
Davis proclaimed several "National Fast"
days during the course of the war to pray
for clemency and forgiveness from God
for the sins of the war. "The National
Fast Day," *Philadelphia Inquirer*, April 29,
1863.

TUESDAY 5

here a little while meeting at [. . .] very few out the groom was not
there to night the grand supper comes off the Sons of St Thomas[41]

WEDNESDAY 6

very stormy tomorrow is exsamination Nellie has not bin up to day
Mary A was up here in all the rain I cut her dress body

THURSDAY, MAY 7, 1863.

Thursday raining I did not go in the morning to the school
exsamination[42] in the afternoon it was very much crowed Cristy had
a speical spelling class in the afternoon for

FRIDAY 8

our benifit the exsercises this morning were very good Sue came in
the morning to see wauford Nellie and anne stoped as they we going

SATURDAY 9

quite a fine day Nellie stoped here as she went up down town this
morning in the evening went to the milleners for my bonnet

SUNDAY, MAY 10, 1863.

[strikethrough][43] very fine day the groom and [. . .] Preach to day
after church we all in a body went to call on the bride bible class

---

41. The Sons of St. Thomas was a "beneficial society" created by members of the St. Thomas (African) Protestant Episcopal Church in 1823. Gatewood, *Aristocrats of Color*, 280; "Institutions for Mutual Relief," in *Making of African American Identity*, http://nationalhumanitiescenter .org/pds/maai/community/text5/ negrosocietiesphil.pdf.

42. Five students took the annual written exams required for graduation at the ICY, answering questions in mathematics (geometry, plane trigonometry, and spherical trigonometry), Latin, and Greek. The *Recorder* published the examinees' scores and their ranking on each of the tests. Caroline LeCount graduated from the school with the highest scores in all three categories. After graduation, LeCount taught at her alma mater and became active in civil rights politics. "Institute for Colored Youth," *Christian Recorder*, May 16, 1863.

43. This entry begins with two and a half lines of crossed-out text. The crossed-out lines appear to be the same entry as on Monday, May 4, 1863, indicating that Davis had written on the wrong page on May 4th.

MONDAY 11

at Mary Joneses clear I noticed the church looke thin in the after noon
No school as usaly there is a [. . .] wonder out about D D J and his

TUESDAY 12

lady allso mr. gibbs becaus he thought he would take a wife to
himself there is a great deal of dissatisfaction in the church about it

WEDNESDAY, MAY 13, 1863.

meeting last night at bundys very few out Perhaps the rain Prevented
saw mr. gibbs was not there we have had another shower to day
Nellie spent the evening with me

THURSDAY 14

another dull day called on miss harris and craig from prinston the rain
Prevented me making several visits i spent the best part of my time
with Nellie

FRIDAY 15

lovely day after the rain I received a sweet littel letter from reading
and his photograph to day I called on magie [. . .] and lizzie brown
this after[noon]

SATURDAY, MAY 16, 1863.

very fine day Nellie was here this morning we had a nice little chat
about matters and things mary stoped in the evening after work i did
not get down home to night

SUNDAY 17

it has bin quite showery all day we had a very heavy thunder storm
this afternoon i have bin quite sick all day have not bin to church
nellie stop after church this morning

MONDAY 18

i answered reading leter to day no one came to see me yesterday but
Nellie I have not seen anything of her to day

TUESDAY, MAY 19, 1863.

very warm to day Nellie stoped a minute to see if I was going to
meeting at Brother adgers[44] we had a happy time mr. fouhex lead
meeting quite a number

WEDNESDAY 20

out cloudy all day Nellie cam up and spent the evening with me she
seems to be my only visiting friend

THURSDAY 21

very buisy all day i did not get out untill after four i went hom then to
nells went over mr. kee and went down to mrs Potters with

FRIDAY, MAY 22, 1863

her in the evening i went to Shiloh anniversery beautiful day Nellie
and went out shoping for mrs potter

SATURDAY 23

very warm day very buisy all day in the evening i went down to
mrs hills to take sues bonnet Nellie went withe me mrs hill Promised
me one of her photog

SUNDAY 24

lovely morning sue and here friend stoped here this morning i do not
like his looks we had a very good sermon this afternoon the bride
was at church

MONDAY, MAY 25, 1863.

we went up to Whites to bible class it was very late the rain
Prevented us liz was ready to take us we had a very interesting class
I ran down home a little

TUESDAY 26

while last night Nellie was up here meeting at browns very few males out
very lively meeting i was very Drowsy i am sorry to say it after meeting

44. Robert and Mary Adger lived in
the Seventh Ward (see the list of people
and institutions in the front matter of
this volume). "William Adger," Penn

Biographies, University of Pennsylvania,
University Archives and Records Center,
http://www.archives.upenn.edu/people/
1800s/adger_wm.html.

WEDNESDAY 27

we went to mrs palmers coming home we met A Jones he came
home with us Nellie spent the evening with me

THURSDAY, MAY 28, 1863.

lovely day liz and i went out visiting we went to call on miss fraler
and mrs reed then went down to the [. . .] ing i went out to see
mrs harris then went

FRIDAY 29

down to the concert[45] it came off very well i have not heard a word
from father i fear they have seceded ry buisy all day have not seen
Nellie mary went to

SATURDAY 30

the concert i went down home found no one there as usal stop at
nellies we had quite a long chat

SUNDAY, MAY 31, 1863.

beutiful morning i went down to church great many out considering
the sermon was very interesting after church we went to see
mrs colegates i stoped

MONDAY JUNE 1

to aunt Jane in the afternoon i spent the evening alone as usall i am
reading the history of Abraham and Jacob very interesting lizie brown
was to see me to day I spent part of

TUESDAY 2

last evening with Nell meeting at Alfred not many there we meet
Vincent at the step he came up home with me EJ was not at meeting
has not bin for som time

45. "[T]he teachers of Bethel Sabbath School" put on a "grand concert" on May 28, 1863, at Sansom Street Hall for the purpose of supporting Wilberforce University. The *Recorder* called the performance "a most praiseworthy object" and celebrated the singing of "Miss Maston, a teacher in the Sabbath School." "Grand Concert," *Christian Recorder*, May 30, 1863.

WEDNESDAY, JUNE 3, 1863.

beutiful day Nellie and miss uhrron called on the bride nell stoped
here in the afternoon she did not com up in the evening Lanine was
here to day Nellie did not get this evening

THURSDAY 4

very pleasent Nellie and i went out it has bin a long time sin we went
shoping togert i went out to germantown about 6 o had a very plea
time vincent

FRIDAY 5

came out for me wich was the pleasent part of the evening Nellie has
not bin up here to day i taken sues corset to harrises

SATURDAY, JUNE 6, 1863.

Nellie stoped here this morning tomorrow is communion i will be
prepared to Partake of the holy sacrement i stoped at Nellies

SUNDAY 7

very cloudy all day i went to church in the afternoon Nellie was sick
and was not out it was communion we had quite a happy time bible
class at mrs chases

MONDAY 8

Mr gibbs did come very buesy all day getting ready for the wedding
Nellie stoped here a little to day Vincent was here this evening
he wanted me to

TUESDAY, JUNE 9, 1863

go to the leeve but i could not make up my mind to neglect my
meeting i felt much better sitting in meeting that i would have bin in

WEDNESDAY 10

the hall very buisey all day i have bin expecting Nellie all the evening
she came late but had bin here early in the evening but could not get
in i was quite

THURSDAY 11

disappointed very Pleasant morning i had a very interesting letter
from Tomy on Monday Nellie and i started out but

FRIDAY, JUNE 12, 1863.

it comenced raining we had to run back down went out later Nellie
was here this morning i wrote to reading this evening vincent came
home with me

SATURDAY 13

last night he semed the same as ever very warm to day i stoped
home sarah seem quite sociable Nellie was not home i staid untill she
cam in

SUNDAY 14

very pleasent in the morning i went to church herd a very good
sermon mr gibbs was very earnest in his remarks in the evening Nell
an Jake cam up

MONDAY, JUNE 15, 1863.

i wrote a long letter to tomy and sent it to the office by Cristy i was
out this afternoon and stoped at Nellie i saw a company of colerd
recruit[46]

TUESDAY 16

ts [recruits] they looked quite war[47] like i was quite sick last night
Nellie was up meeting at [. . .] very good meeting great many out
mr White frighten us by saying

---

46. In response to intelligence that
reported the concentration of Robert E.
Lee's Army of Northern Virginia on the
state's southern border, Governor Andrew
Curtin issued a call for men to report to
the defense of the state. The next day,
June 17, 1863, 150 men of color boarded
trains in Philadelphia and traveled to Harrisburg to report for duty but returned the
next day, after Governor Curtin refused
their service. Prominent among the
rejected recruits were men associated with
the Banneker Institute. Many of these
men joined the 3rd USCT. "Local Affairs,"
Public Ledger, June 17, 1863, 1; Dubin and
Biddle, *Tasting Freedom*, 292–93.

47. By June 16, the papers confirmed
Philadelphians' worst fears—they were in
the midst of a Confederate invasion. Emilie also elaborated on these events in the
memoranda section of her diary for 1863.
"The New Rebel Movement," *Philadelphia
Inquirer*, June 16, 1863.

FIGURE 8 Octavius Catto. Octavius Catto taught at the Institute for Colored Youth and was among the black men who volunteered to defend Pennsylvania during the Confederate invasion of June 1863. Image from *Portrait Album of Well Known 19th-Century African American Men of Philadelphia, 1865–1885*, P.9304, The Library Company of Philadelphia.

WEDNESDAY 17

that a great many of his dear frins expected to go to ware [war]
at 12 o clock after meeting i asked who he said all the boyes to day
has bin the most

THURSDAY, JUNE 18, 1863.

Exciting i ever witness we went to see the boyes start for harrisburg
i left home about 11 o clock it was almost 12 when i came home this
morning the first thing I heard

FRIDAY 19

was that the boyes had bin sent back i feel glad and sorry last night
we had quite a Disloyal meeting about mr gibbs the trustees were
about to turn mr gibbs right

SATURDAY 20[48]

out of the church the meeting was posponed it was almost 12 when
we left the church the boyes are still talking about going to ware
[war][49]

SUNDAY, JUNE 21, 1863.

rather showery i went to church in the afternoon herd a very good
sermon we all are so thankful that our boyes are all hom again bible
class cosed this evening

MONDAY 22

the attendance was very large we closed to meet in october if we are
spared sue stayed with me all night and went out [. . .] this morning
Nellie

48. Emilie notes other events on this date in the memoranda pages at the end of her diary, including the marriage of Sarah Thomas.

49. Section 2 of the Militia Act of July 17, 1862, allowed black men to join as federal soldiers. Massachusetts was the first state to begin forming black regiments, recruiting and filling black regiments early in 1863. Recruiting began in Pennsylvania in mid-1863, and Camp William Penn began training black recruits. By the end of the war, 11,000 black men from Pennsylvania had served in the USCT. Binder, "Pennsylvania Negro Regiments," 383–417.

TUESDAY 23

was up here a little while i feel so worried about Father[50] we had
a very happy meeting to night Johns lead the meeting everyone
semed to

WEDNESDAY, JUNE 24, 1863.

to enjoy it mrs gibbs was there [. . .] very buisy to day Nellie came
up and staid untill 10 clo go we had a Pleasent chat as usal about
cristy

THURSDAY 25

Beautiful day i went to harrises stoped at Duglasses an gordanes spent
a little while with Nell then went down to affects to ellie spence
i spent quite

FRIDAY 26

an agreable time with the girls came hom about 15-past nine cristy
came up with me Reading spent the morning with me his visit was
pleasent

SATURDAY, JUNE 27, 1863.

Nell had a letter from reading Sarah Thomas is married it seems like
a dream but it is reality Nellie was up this morning i [. . .] there thi
afternoon rach come in and plai

SUNDAY 28

d [plaid] a little while lovely day i went to church Johns preached for
us his sermon was very good after church went to mrs colgates &
palmer & mary Jones I went down to Sunday school and [. . .]

MONDAY 29

[. . .] to teach her class i sent a letter to Father last night To day has
bin the most exciting day i has witness refugees[51] are comin from all
the towns this side of

50. Emilie was right to worry about
her father's safety, as rebel soldiers kid-
napped hundreds of free blacks and sold
them into slavery in June and July 1863.
Harrold, *Border War*, 209–10.

51. Refugees, both black and white,
fled in advance of Lee's June–July
invasion of south-central Pennsylvania.
Many Pennsylvanians of color fled to Philadelphia, where they hoped to find safety.

TUESDAY, JUNE 30, 1863.

harrisburg the greates excitement Prevails I am all most sick worrin about father the city is considered in danger[52] meeting at mrs o neils [. . .] feeling mr guy lead there seems to be a better spirit among

WEDNESDAY, JULY 1

our peopel the excitement is not quite so great to day Johns started for reading to day vincent is perfectly wild with excitement The boyes have all volenteerd[53] Nellie

THURSDAY 2

cam up and spent quite a pleasent evening I went down hom found things quite agreeable in the afternoon i went to see mrs burn spent the evening with Doll

FRIDAY, JULY 3, 1863.

Cristy did not com up last night Vincent cam home with me what i would if he was not about i do not kow Rube com up this morning he left about half Pas one for

SATURDAY 4

st. louis colid soldiers has become quite a matter of course the fourth[54] has bin very quiet up in our part of the city i was down hom a little while very few [. . .]

Emilie was excited about seeing the refugees, but their stories likely aggravated her fears for her father's safety. Emilie also notes this event in the memoranda pages of her diary for 1863. "The Skeedaddle from York," *Philadelphia Inquirer*, June 20, 1863; "Exodus of Colored Population," *Philadelphia Inquirer*, June 20, 1863.

52. Although Philadelphians believed that Lee's army was destined to strike at their city, Harrisburg was at greater risk during the Army of Northern Virginia's monthlong invasion of the state. Calderhead, "Philadelphia in Crisis," 142–55.

53. Although the War Department created the Bureau of Colored Troops in May 1863, black Pennsylvanians were only permitted to enlist the following month, after Secretary of War Edwin Stanton wrote a letter ordering Pennsylvania Major General Darius Couch in Harrisburg to accept black recruits. Gallman, *Mastering Wartime*, 46–47.

54. Though Emilie notes a quiet Fourth of July in Philadelphia, it was an exceptionally memorable day in the war. July 4, 1863, featured twin Union victories at Gettysburg and Vicksburg. After a three-day battle at Gettysburg, General Lee and the Army of Northern Virginia retreated back across the Potomac River on July 4. General Grant and the Army of the Tennessee ended their siege of Vicksburg, accepting Confederate surrender on July 4.

SUNDAY 5

quite a rainy day i went to church very few out we had very good
sermon after church i spent part of the time home

MONDAY, JULY 6, 1863.

and the evening in Nellies how i miss bible class Vincent cam home
with me Nellie was up here to day

TUESDAY 7

very dull day meeting at mrs holins very few out great rejocing here
the surrender of Vicksburg[55] to night mrs gibbs and lucy came up to

WEDNESDAY 8

Nellies after meeting Mrs Buzard leaft for cope [Cape] My [May] This
morning very heavy storm it rained in torrents all day

THURSDAY, JULY 9, 1863.

very dull day it rained rained hard soon after i went out i received a
liter from Father to day i went around to marys i spent the

FRIDAY 10

evening with nell cristy did not com i have a letter from tomy cristy
and st all [. . .] go past with recruits[56] Sue was in tonight she looked

SATURDAY 11

lovely John stoped for her very buisy getting the folks ready to go
away i went down hom Sarah was quite talketive

---

55. The people of Philadelphia
erupted into celebration when the news of
Grant's victory at Vicksburg reached the
city. The celebration included fireworks
and the word "Victory" spelled out by
gaslights above the Union League on
Broad Street. Gallman, *Mastering Wartime*,
107–8.

56. The soldiers Emilie mentions
may have been trained at Camp William
Penn. The camp opened on June 26,
1863, eight miles north of Philadelphia

in Cheltenham, adjacent to the home of
abolitionists James and Lucretia Mott.
Soldiers from Camp William Penn were
known to parade the streets of Philadelphia. The *Recorder* described one such
parade on October 10, 1863. Recruitment
for the first regiment of black soldiers was
taking place as Emilie wrote this entry.
Binder, "Pennsylvania Negro Regiments,"
383–417; Wert, "Camp William Penn," 340–
41; Gallman, *Mastering Wartime*, 47–49.

FIGURE 9   Camp William Penn. Camp William Penn opened near Cheltenham, Pennsylvania, in June 1863. Eleven thousand troops were trained there, among them the 26th U.S. Colored Volunteer Infantry pictured here on parade in 1865. Emilie noted the appearance of colored troops in Philadelphia on several occasions. The National Archives and Records Administration, 165-C-692.

SUNDAY, JULY 12, 1863.

quite pleasent this morning i went down to church Mr Collen preached for us he gave us quite a milatary discourse i went down to Sunday school Vincent came

MONDAY 13 [57]

up to see me in the evening he paid quite a pleasant visit very busy all day Nellie stoped a little while i went to see about a situation till we

TUESDAY 14

get it very dull morning Mrs. Powel did not get off she went to Father and sent him some money meeting at Stewarts very Pleasant even [. . .]

WEDNESDAY, JULY 15, 1863.

was not there this has bin quiet [quite] a holiday i have not seen Nellie to day i do not like the prospect of having no work[58] all sum

THURSDAY 16

mer [summer] very fine morning the folks go off i am happy to say i stop i [. . .] untill most nine o clock i staid in Nellies all

FRIDAY 17

night i am all most tired of doing nothing ready i went up to buzards after [. . .] things [. . .]

SATURDAY, JULY 18, 1863.

me som lunch wich was very nice it rained so hard last night i did not go to meeting to day i have bin busy helping to clean up i do not

SUNDAY 19

feel so idle I went to church in the morning very few out in the afternoon i went to Sunday school i taught Liz and Nells classes after church Mary and I went

57. Though Emilie does not mention it here, in the memoranda pages at the end of her diary she comments on the deadly draft riots in New York City in July 1863.

58. In the summer, Emilie worked as a domestic just outside the city. She worked for the Harris family in 1863. African American women often supported themselves by cleaning, cooking, and caring for other women's children. Jones, *American Work*, 280–81.

MONDAY 20

down to offer us certain days mother with in the evening Sarah duglos [Douglass][59] and i went to cristys to [. . .] bin a lovely day i have

TUESDAY, JULY 21, 1863.

bin busy sewing all day This morning it rained quite hard clear in the afternoon meeting was at our house very good meeting

WEDNESDAY 22

Pop Stewart is seriously impressed Nellie was not with us all day Sunday very busy all day went around to Maryes then stoped at Nellies

THURSDAY 23

very warm Nellie and i went out shoping stoped to see Lizzie at 16th and walnut very busy sewing part of the evening

FRIDAY, JULY 24, 1863.

very pleasant day i stoped to [. . .] Nellie then spent the afternoon in at 16th Walnut about five Nellie + i went up to whites and staid untill meeting time i

SATURDAY 25

spent quite a pleasent visit i had the pleasure of seeing some rebels[60] that were opisite home all day not very well

SUNDAY 26

very pleasent i went to church all day had a stranger to preach for us in the after noon in the evening Nellie Cristy and i went

MONDAY, JULY 27, 1863.

to Sues spent a very plesent evening i spent part of the morning at Maryes she is better after super Nellie and went on to Duglasses[61] i went to

---

59. This Sarah Douglass may have been the stepdaughter of Sarah Mapps Douglass, an active member of the PFASS and a teacher at the ICY. If this is the correct Sarah Douglass, she was twenty-three years old in 1863, an age-appropriate peer for Emilie Davis. Dunbar, *Fragile Freedom*, 70–71.

60. It is possible that Emilie caught a glimpse of Confederate prisoners who were sent to Fort Mifflin, located beside the Delaware River. Fort Mifflin served as a prison during the Civil War. Dorwart, *Fort Mifflin*, 116–18.

61. Sarah Douglass had seven siblings: Elizabeth (twenty-six years old),

TUESDAY 28

see the soldiers come home[62] meeting at Nellies quit a suden death
Mrs. Stewart died[63] this afternoon i can hardly realize it very nice
meeting i received a letter from Nathen to day

WEDNESDAY 29

to day is the great day out at the [. . .] i did not go i had a letter from
Alfred I was to go to gertrudes but the rain

THURSDAY, JULY 30, 1863.

Prevented us very busy all day at home very dull day in the evening
i went up to buzards then around to Miss whom Mary is still sick

FRIDAY 31

to day is the eventful day they begin to Draft in the seventh ward[64]
Alfred and EJ are both drafted Mary is quite worried[65] i hope he will
not have

Mary (twenty), Caroline (eighteen), Francis (sixteen), Lacontena (twelve), Anna (eleven), and Joseph (nine). With a full house and a graceful and erudite stepmother, the Douglasses' home would have been a welcoming place to visit. 1860 United States Federal Census, Philadelphia Ward 5 Southern Division, Philadelphia, Pennsylvania, roll M653_1155, page 563, image 569, family history library film 805155.

62. Women of color were known to visit family and friends at Camp William Penn. In a letter to the chief of the Bureau of Colored Troops, the chairman of the Supervisory Committee of Colored Troops, Thomas Webster, wrote that he saw 120 women at the base during an inspection. Thomas Webster to CW Foster, March 22, 1864. Letters sent to Camp William Penn, Provost Marshal General's Bureau (Civil War) Records Group 110, National Archives at Philadelphia. Also see

"Colored People and the War," *Christian Recorder*, October 1, 1864, for a description of a visit to Camp William Penn by a black man and two black women.

63. Amanda Steward died on July 28, 1863, of "carditis." Her funeral was held on August 1. "Pennsylvania, Philadelphia City Death Certificates, 1803–1915," index and images, FamilySearch, https://familysearch.org/pal:/MM9.1.1/JX6K-XX8 (accessed May 8, 2013), Amanda Steward, 1863.

64. Although unpopular, Philadelphia's draft was quite orderly. "The Draft Not Suspended," *North American and United States Gazette* (Philadelphia), July 16, 1863; "The Draft in the Eighteenth Ward—All Quiet in That Part of the City," *Philadelphia Inquirer*, July 14, 1863; "The Draft," *Philadelphia Inquirer*, July 15, 1863.

65. Life was difficult for soldiers' wives like Mary. The death rate for

SATURDAY, AUGUST 1

to go Elijah is over the Mrs. Steward was buried yesterday Elijah got a
[. . .] and we all would I stoped up to hazards

SUNDAY, AUGUST 2, 1863.

I think this has bin one of the warmest dayes we have had this
summer i went down to Sunday school in the morning Nellie was not
out in the evening

MONDAY 3

i was in to Maryes she had company Nellie treated very strangely
i cant acount for it Mary is still sick and have not heard from Alfred

TUESDAY 4

fine day meeting at [. . .] this evening at whites i shoped at hazerds
Nellie did not go very few out after meeting i went arou

WEDNESDAY, AUGUST 5, 1863.

nd [around] to choser to day the great picnic comes off I went with
Nellie to the office we did not get started until after 8 when we go
over sue found to our disappointment they had all gone and left

THURSDAY 6

us and we did not know where to go we staid at the wharf until after
10 we did not get any berries and was disappointed in the borgon
very busy all day in the evening we went

FRIDAY 7

up to agusteses yesterday my thanks giving day i went to church in
the afternoon very few out

---

military-age men may have been as high
as ten times the average. Wives argued
with their husbands over enlisting and
reenlisting. Mary's worry about her
husband, Alfred, was likely compounded
by her own illness and her fears about
how she would care for her son, Frank,
in Alfred's absence. Hacker, "Census-Based
Count," 312n3.

SATURDAY, AUGUST 8, 1863.

[. . .] Nellie [. . .] girl she [. . .] Desired we had quite a nice
meeting last night Sarah got off to day after she had gone i found out
someone had

SUNDAY 9

bin in my trunk i found it was Ellie Williams very warm day Nellie
spent the day in our house she is very worshipping i went to church
all day Mary is quite sick to day

MONDAY 10

i was away to choses a little while last night quite warm i spent part
of the morning with mary I wrote to Sarah and Alfred yesterday

TUESDAY, AUGUST 11, 1863.

yesterday i fixed those things for father EJ sent them to day for me
Mrs. Harris came for me to go out with her to the country i promised
to go on Thursday meeting

WEDNESDAY 12

at modissons liz and i were the only females there we had a nice little
meeting I have bin very busy getting ready to go away Mary had a
letter from Alfred she was over here to day

THURSDAY 13

Bill Alger was married on last tuesday night Nellie an gorge went
to the reception very pleasent to day this afternoon i heard from
Harrises i feel very loth to go just at this time

FRIDAY, AUGUST 14, 1863.

Nellies in trouble and mary sick i had a very pleasent day out with
mr harris every thing looks natural mrs harris goes away to day
i wrote a long letter[66]

---

66. As she prepared to leave Philadelphia for her job in the East Falls section of the city in August 1863, Emilie became very anxious about leaving her friends and family, especially as Alfred had just been drafted and because Alfred's wife, Mary, was ill. Emilie wrote many letters over the summer to try to keep abreast of the affairs of family and friends.

SATURDAY 15

to nellie and sent it in town to day i has bin very busy all day but got
along very well I has a caught a bad cold in my head i feel quit under

SUNDAY 16

the weather it is quite pleasent to day i did not feel well enough to go
to church i have felt quite sick all day i spent the morning in reading
and sleeping in the

MONDAY, AUGUST 17, 1863.

evening harriet and took a walk we had a lovely shower last night
it is very pleasant to day I expect a letter from nellie to day i shall be
disappointed if i do not get one the day has past

TUESDAY 18

i had no letter yet i am still looking for one to day I have had quite a
nice time out here so far if i only felt well i would be glad I shall miss
meeting to night it is the first time i have missed a night for a long

WEDNESDAY 19

time no letter yet from how lovely day the area is so sweet and
pure Theodore came out and never stoped at the house I have had a
pleasent time so far out here

THURSDAY, AUGUST 20, 1863

no letter yet i think my friends have forsaken me very warm I have
bin quite busy all day it just a week to day since i came out here
Mr Stimer was over to see us this evening

FRIDAY 21

very warm day at last i have a letter from Nelli she has bin to Cape
May she is in good spirits everything is all right between her and her
mother I have bin quite sick all day not ab

SATURDAY 22

le [able] to do my work I sent a note in to EJ on Thursday i hope he
will answer it soon i have bin sick all day i hope i will be able to go to
church tomorrow morning

SUNDAY, AUGUST 23, 1863.

very warm day I went to church in the morning heard a very good
sermon young white minister that spoke reminded me of John in the
afternoon i did not spend is profitable as i mig

MONDAY 24

ht [might] in the evening we went to prayer meeting had a spirited
meeting our party were the only colored people there there was about
four of us to day has bin very windy i am going to wait

TUESDAY 25

to see if Nellie will write before i answer her letter very pleasant
morning I received three from hom to day one from lizz and nell and
EJ we had a very heavy shower this evening

WEDNESDAY, AUGUST 26, 1863.

quite cool to day I have written three notes hom to day one to Nell
Liz and EJ quite lovly out here Ephraim cam here this morning and
stay a very long time i was almost

THURSDAY 27

chilled through standing out on the piazza i have bin busy all day
mr harris is in town harriet Theodore and I went down to the Falls[67]
for ice cream[68] but

FRIDAY 28

We came back as we went ephraim gave us 50 ct to get some ice
cream very busy all day i hardly had time to think of home the
weather is

67. The "falls" referenced here are
the Falls of the Schuylkill River, near the
Falls Bridge by the Laurel Hill Cemetery
at Thirty-Sixth and Allegheny Streets
in Philadelphia. The dam at Fairmount,
constructed in 1821, raised the water
level enough to eliminate the falls, but
the name of the neighborhood remained.
Today, the area is known as East Falls.
Jackson, *Encyclopedia*, 644–45.

68. Philadelphians of color did not
generally take for granted such luxuries
as going out with a friend for ice cream.
In the summer of 1857, Charlotte Forten
and a friend were refused service at three
ice cream salons in a row before they gave
up. Grimké, June 17–25, 1857, *Journals*,
22–23.

SATURDAY, AUGUST 29, 1863.

so cool i expect hazards will be home before i am ready for them to has bin quite pleasent very windy I should like to be home tomorrow to go to church it seems

SUNDAY 30

so long since i came out here to has bin a lovely day I have not bin to church i have not bin well and my arm is so lame that i am unable to raise it to comb my hair I want to go this evening

MONDAY 31

i went to church last night and heard a good sermon Johnson girls came over and spent the evening with us to day has bin very pleasent in the evening harriet Ephraim and i went over to with

TUESDAY, SEPTEMBER 1, 1863.

we met some of the familyes People i believe i saw I received a letter from E J Poor Mary is very sick yet i feel very ansious about her no word from Nell this evening harriet

WEDNESDAY 2

and i went over to Johnsons we had nice fun i have just finished a letter to E J and one to Mary Poor girl she is so ill I feel quite worried about her

THURSDAY 3

very Pleasant to day i have bin very busy all day sewing i have not heard a word from Nell i expect a letter tomorrow harriet and i have had grand bin this week

FRIDAY, SEPTEMBER 4, 1863.

very Pleasant day no letter from Nellie what can the matter be today we had a grand romp out on the town rachel Jonston came over in the afternoon and ephriam will the rest in

SATURDAY 5

the evening James went off and locked us all i the kitchen Harriet leaves us this morning very sorry i am Rachel and i went to the cars with her then went to West Phila to see [. . .]

SUNDAY 6

Fulmer We had a Pleasent drive lovely day I have bin unable to go to church this morning how i would like to be in town it is commiun Sunday i went to church in the evening had very interesting

MONDAY, SEPTEMBER 7, 1863.

sermon The widower was with me quite Pleasent to day lizzie come out to day for coock i am so glad she brought me a letter from Nell poor girl she has had her [. . .]

TUESDAY 8

Troubls since i left agatha has gone to washington Jay go with her i have bin very busy all day i had i letter from EJ telling me he had spent all or nearly all

WEDNESDAY 9

of my money very incuraging last night had all went over to Johnsons we had a good bit of fun but i think it is the last time i will climb mt hill

THURSDAY, SEPTEMBER 10, 1863.

very fine day katie and i went carrige riding with James Kate got hurt I had a letter from harrriet tonight I am

FRIDAY 11

I had a letter from brother to day Theodore went home to day we will miss him much he is so full of fun Johnsons girls com over this evening rachel has

SATURDAY 12

not gone[69] hom yet harriet has bin gone one weeke to day i have bin as busy as a bee all day mr and mrs harris and mary had a narrow

---

69. Emilie's list of September departures suggests that some of these people were employed at the same household as Emilie and that as they left, Emilie's work increased, or she became anxious to return to Philadelphia with them.

SUNDAY, SEPTEMBER 13, 1863.

escape last night the buggy was broken and they were thrown out but did not get hurt very Pleasent after the rain I went to church in the morning and heard a very

MONDAY 14

good sermon no church in the evening I had a letter EJ to informing me that alfred had gone to Cannada[70] i am very sorry Mary is still quite sick

TUESDAY 15

very dull day i am almost tired of the country Barnes cam and no letter from [. . .] i was disappointed i feel very ansious

WEDNESDAY, SEPTEMBER 16, 1863.

to be home I received a letter from Nellie to day it was quite a ledger but the same had news about marys health received/answered EJs and Nellies letters to

THURSDAY 17

day i have bin very busy all day it is very lonsome out here on a rainy day i went up to barns yesterday for my letter met Ephriam he invited me to go over to

FRIDAY 18

see Mrs Michael on Sunday i think i will go to day has bin a very stormy dreary day the rain was very hard i sent some money home for Nelly to dispose

SATURDAY, SEPTEMBER 19, 1863.

it is quite cold to day we had to have fire in the furnace I only have a few more dayes oute here i feel ansious to be home there is no Place like home

---

70. The purpose of Alfred's trip to Canada is unclear; however, he was back in Philadelphia to enlist in the Navy on October 27, 1863. National Park Service, "Civil War Soldiers and Sailors System," http://www.nps.gov/civilwar/search-sailors-detail.htm?sailors_id=Dav0008.

SUNDAY 20

if it is ever so humble this morning i went to church it was quite cool in the afternoon Ephriam taken me over to Mrs Michael we had quite a Pleasant Drive he

MONDAY 21

was quite devoted to me the weather begins to be cool it is moon light no it is not so Dreary

TUESDAY, SEPTEMBER 22, 1863.

I received a note from Poll and a letter from Mary Jane she is quite sick both in body and in mind she tells us her husband has found the blessing and she is

WEDNESDAY 23

seeking for it i trust Nell tells me i have a neice i have another long and interesting letter from Nell to day she sends me all the news cristie and

THURSDAY 24

her are on the outs i am very sorry but i can not help it i will have to take him to task when i go home last night

FRIDAY, SEPTEMBER 25, 1863.

lizzie ephraim and i went over to rutheys i have a letter from hariet to day i expected one from EJ but i did not yet

SATURDAY 26

very busy as usol it is lovely to day I had bin troubled with a sore eye ever since wednesday night i will be so glad when the time comes for me to

SUNDAY 27

go home very pleasent to day i went to church heard a good sermon i have not bin well Ephriam came over in the afternoon in the evening we went

MONDAY, SEPTEMBER 28, 1863.

down to the falls to the methodist church to day has bin blue
monday i did not feel like work gorge fulmer was here singing for our
amusement he was [. . .]

TUESDAY 29

as usal I have bin waiting patiently for a letter but no letter came
I expect to go home this very week

WEDNESDAY 30

very fine day i walked up to thorneses to see if he had brought me a
letter but he had not in the evening barnes came over with one for end

THURSDAY, OCTOBER 1, 1863.

my time is up to day i have bin very busy washing [. . .] to take a
walk with Ephriam but we were too tired i answered nellies

FRIDAY 2

last night this is my last week out here i hope Nell is very ansious for
me to come home Alfred has come home cristy and nell are acting

SATURDAY 3

friendly yet mrs harris wants me to stay another week she has heard
from fanny she wont be home for school

SUNDAY, OCTOBER 4, 1863.

monthes very pleasent to day i went to church in the morning heard
an excelent sermon in the afternoon lizzie ephriam and went to see
Mr Packer he has

MONDAY 5

a lovely place he gave us some beautiful flowers I bid my Dear
Ephriam farewell last night i had bin busy getting ready to go home
i sent my things to day

TUESDAY 6

mrs harris treated me like a lady she said she was sorry she had to
part with me I leave to day Nell was delighted to see me i stoped at
hazards [. . .]

WEDNESDAY, OCTOBER 7, 1863.

went down home sarah received me very well Poor mary is very ill
i do not think she will be here long i have not seen alfred yet Nelly
and i we

THURSDAY 8

nt [went] out shoping i bought a cloak to day i have bin triming my
bonnet i am waiting and sarah and mary both I was up to hazards this
evening

FRIDAY 9

very busy all day poor mary is no better i expect to go with her to see
a german doct liz and i was out shoping we went to meeting in the
even

SATURDAY, OCTOBER 10, 1863.

ing [evening] very few out I went up to the Doctors with mary he
sayes he can do nothing for her her lungs is too far gone now sad
i feel very ansious

SUNDAY 11

about her lovely day i did not go to church this morning I went in the
afternoon i spend the greater part of my time with mary i stoped at
mrs brister

MONDAY 12

for nelly she is very good spirited i went to hazards morning every
thing is at S. Sevens stoped home and out at mary

TUESDAY, OCTOBER 13, 1863.

i do not think she is long for this world if she was only Perpard i did
not go to meeting to night it being elections night[71]

WEDNESDAY 14

very busy today as usole to night is the party out at Clayes i think of
going i went to the party and enjoyed myself nicely

71. Elections were held in the city on
October 13. "Election To-Day," *Philadelphia
Press*, October 13, 1863, 2.

THURSDAY 15

Vincent was there and came home with us quite dull today spent the greater part of my time with mary she seemed to be in a very good frame of mind she said she would

FRIDAY, OCTOBER 16, 1863.

like someone to talk with here mrs Jordan promised to send one of her minesters wich she did very rainy all day Cristie is still pufing our frendsh with Nell he has not bin

SATURDAY 17

there for foure weeks Beautiful day i have bin looking for nell of the morning meal harriet was here miss mccormick died yesterday mary seems no better we had singing and

SUNDAY 18

praying last evening lovely day like spring i was out in the morning Rachel is acting Frenchy I am mad me furious this moring EJ and i called on the Baid Mrs Mareck

MONDAY, OCTOBER 19, 1863.

she is slept nicely I stoped to see mary she is still very ill i fear she will not get over this atacck Nellie and the girls spent the evening at seymours i

TUESDAY 20

felt so bad i did go Nell stoped in as she went up to the furneal I wrote up to father Sunday meeting at riders Nell did not go she went over to see mary

WEDNESDAY 21

Alfred went up to the Provost marshals they would not exempt[72] him I feel quite ansious about him i expected Nellie here to night but she did

72. Having returned from Canada, Alfred asked to be exempted from the draft out of concern for his wife's failing health and worry about who would care for his child in his absence. With the Confederacy threatening to execute members of the USCT who fell into its hands, Alfred's fears about leaving his son an orphan were well founded. However, because his wife was still alive, he would

THURSDAY, OCTOBER 22, 1863.

not come I have bin quite sick all day mary is a little she think I spent the afternoon with her in the evening Nellie and i went down to Gertruds

FRIDAY 23

we spent a pleasent evening vincent was to come down but did not get here we met him cristie was up here this evening we had quite a serious

SATURDAY 24

talk Nell was up here this morning poor girl she looks badly i can fell for here but i hope they will be reconciled to each other ever long

SUNDAY, OCTOBER 25, 1863.

very cold and dreary Nellie quite sick not over all day Sue was in town I went to church in the afternoon heard a very good sermon i spent part of the evening with mary and the

MONDAY 26

other part with Nell she seemed so low I hurte very fine day yesterday Sue gorge and i stoped at aunt Janes poor charlie is very ill we did not go up to see him Nell is down

TUESDAY 27

there i stoped to see mary she is very ill poor Charlie died this morning at 1 o clock he died beautiful meeting in [. . .] very few out but

WEDNESDAY, OCTOBER 28, 1863.

we had a happy time after meeting i went down to aunt Janes poor mary is very ill to day Alfred went on the ship[73] to day i felt so badly about it to think he has to go away

not have been eligible for exemption in October 1863. Meier, "Civil War Draft Records," http://www.archives.gov/publications/prologue/1994/winter/civil-war-draft-records.html.

73.   Alfred enlisted in the U.S. Navy on October 27, 1863, served on the USS *Mount Vernon*, and mustered out on December 31, 1864. Although the federal Militia Act of 1792 excluded black men

CUTTING OUT OF THE SOUTHERN SCHOONER "ALIA," OFF DE FILE, BY THE BOATS OF THE U. S. STEAM FRIGATE NIAGARA, ASSISTED BY THE U. S. STEAMER MOUNT VERNON, JULY 5, 1861.—FROM A SKETCH BY AN OFFICER OF THE EXPEDITION.—SEE PAGE 116

FIGURE 10 USS *Mount Vernon*. Emilie's brother, Alfred, served on the USS *Mount Vernon*, a steamship that, by 1863, was part of the U.S. blockade off the coast of North Carolina. In this photo, the USS *Mount Vernon* is shown assisting the USS *Niagara*. Naval History and Heritage Command, Washington, D.C., NH 59145.

THURSDAY 29

Just as this time when mary is so ill Alfred was home to day Mr gibbs was to see mary this afternoon he said she expressed a hope that her sins had bin forgiven Nell and

FRIDAY 30

i spent part of the evening with her then we called to see mrs palmer then went to see aunt Jane Charlie was buried this morning he had a

SATURDAY, OCTOBER 31, 1863.

very respectable funeral Mr gibbs was slighed he was not invited to the funeral Mr Catos remarks were very good lizzie has bin dead three years to day mary is very ill tonight

SUNDAY 1

lovely day i went to church in the morning heard a very good sermon stoped at mrs gibbs and at millses I spent the rest of my time with mary she is very ill

MONDAY 2

very fine day i went down to see mary found her very ill in truley helpless stoped over home and told sarah in the afternoon Nell came up for me Mary was diei

TUESDAY, NOVEMBER 3, 1863.

ng [dying] i went down and staid with her she died[74] last night about 7 oclock she died very calm she was ready Alfred did not get to see her very long all day cleaning up the house

---

from service in the U.S. Army, the Navy never barred black men from service. When the Civil War began, several hundred black men were already in service. At least 18,000 African American men served in the Navy during the war. They made up approximately 20 percent of the Navy's total force—double the proportion of black soldiers in the Army. National Park Service, "Civil War Soldiers and Sailors System," http://www.nps

.gov/civilwar/search-sailors-detail.htm ?sailors_id=Dav0008; Reidy, "Black Men in Navy Blue," http://www.archives.gov/ publications/prologue/2001/fall/black -sailors-1.html.

74. Five days after her husband reported for the U.S. Navy, Mary Davis died, leaving little Frank's future undetermined. Sick since July, Mary died of "consumption of lungs," according to her death certificate, on November 2.

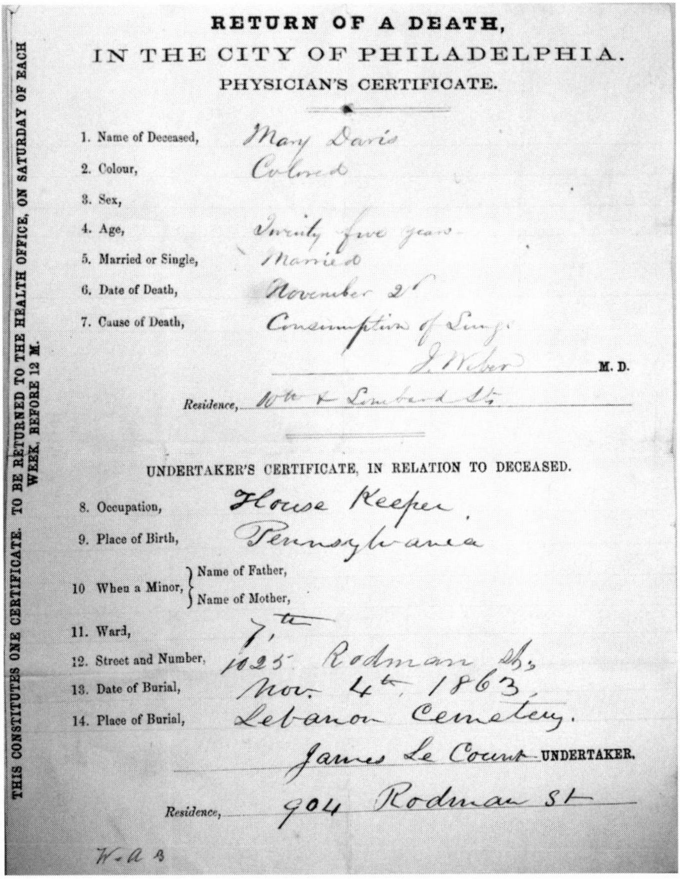

THIS CONSTITUTES ONE CERTIFICATE. TO BE RETURNED TO THE HEALTH OFFICE, ON SATURDAY OF EACH WEEK, BEFORE 12 M.

RETURN OF A DEATH,

IN THE CITY OF PHILADELPHIA.

PHYSICIAN'S CERTIFICATE.

1. Name of Deceased, Mary Davis
2. Colour, Colored
3. Sex,
4. Age, Twenty five years
5. Married or Single, Married
6. Date of Death, November 2d
7. Cause of Death, Consumption of Lungs

J. Weber M. D.

Residence, 10th & Lombard St.

UNDERTAKER'S CERTIFICATE, IN RELATION TO DECEASED.

8. Occupation, House Keeper.
9. Place of Birth, Pennsylvania

10 When a Minor, Name of Father, Name of Mother,

11. Ward, 7th
12. Street and Number, 1025 Rodman St.
13. Date of Burial, Nov. 4th, 1863.
14. Place of Burial, Lebanon Cemetery.

James Le Count UNDERTAKER.

Residence, 904 Rodman St

W. A. B.

FIGURE 11 Mary Davis's death certificate. Mary Davis, Emilie's sister-in-law, died a few days after her husband, Alfred, reported for service in the U.S. Navy. With no parents to care for him, seven-year-old Frank was taken to a Quaker orphanage. Mary Davis, Return of Death, burial date: November 4, 1863, Lebanon Cemetery. Courtesy of Philadelphia City Archives.

WEDNESDAY 4

mary J and I poor Mary is to be buried to day no word of Alfred Poor little Frank is left an orphan Mr Gibbs attended the funral Frank[75] went home

THURSDAY 5

and fixed the thinghs Nell mrs sisco and [. . .] And ther mother were there i went to hazards to day they seem to simpythize with me I have

FRIDAY, NOVEMBER 6, 1863.

bin so very busy since i came up here I have hardly had time to think Mary Sue was in yesterday I was down home a little while to day Frank seems to be

SATURDAY 7

quite contented John came home he came running in here yesterday i was delighted to see him Nell and went up to the doctors this morning he was not ther

SUNDAY 8

Pleasent in the morning I was not out we had an excellent sermon in the afternoon bible class commences this evening at Mr Gibbs very

MONDAY, NOVEMBER 9, 1863.

nice class Nell was not there or Vincent Tom was up a little while Nell stoped she is still very disconsolate I pitty her for I have suffered the same i finished my bonnet[76] to night

---

Dr. George B. Wood wrote in 1858 that tuberculosis (or consumption) was often caused by "insufficient food, confinement, want of fresh air and exercise, habitual exposure to cold, sensual excesses, great loss of blood or other depletion." Wood noted that in colder climates, tuberculosis particularly affected the young and the elderly, and he remarked that "[n]egroes are . . . more disposed to the disease than the whites." Wood, *Treatise*, 115–19.

75. On December 7, EJ turned over custody and care of seven-year-old Frank

to the Association for the Care of Colored Orphans. After his mother's death and his father's departure, this might have been Frank's best chance to go to school; alternatively, the "shelter," as it was called, would send children out to work. Frank Davis, December 7, 1863, Association for the Care of Colored Orphans Records, 1822–1979 (Record Group 4/008), ser. 3, Friends Historical Library of Swarthmore College.

76. African American women in the audience for the American Anti-Slavery

TUESDAY 10

very cold and blustery tomy spent quite a while with me i love to
have him come up to see me meeting up to Whites great many out
we had quite a nice meeting

WEDNESDAY 11

very busy today tomy was up today he comes up nearly every day Nell
was up and spent the evening EJ worrering [worrying] me about Frank

THURSDAY, NOVEMBER 12, 1863.

very pleasent to day tom cam up to go out with me but got tired of
waiting i went down to [. . .] spent the best part of the evening there
went

FRIDAY 13

to see Mr Lively he was not home Tomy and i went to have his
potograph [photograph] taken he gave me a Portfolio his and a set of
guitar strings

SATURDAY 14

very busy all day Nell came up to go with me to the doctor but i
could not go i went in the afternoon i went down home this evening

SUNDAY, NOVEMBER 15, 1863.

very rainy morning morning I went down to church very few out
Cristy was not there Vincent came in just as church was out he has
forsaken me Nell was up this evening

MONDAY 16

very dull today tom went down on the see [. . .] ship this morning
the girls went to see Mr Lively today to see if would teach the school
he promised to let

Society convention on December 4
dressed sharply, donning bonnets and
dresses as they listened to the various
speakers. Perhaps Emilie made her bonnet
in anticipation of the event, which she
seems to have attended. Some newspaper
coverage was dismissive of the meeting,
as is evidenced by this headline: "The Abolition Convention. Meeting of a Mutual
Admiration Club. Semi-Feminine Men
and Strong-Minded Women," *Daily Age*
(Philadelphia), December 4, 1863.

TUESDAY 17

us know on Wednesday tonight the glory presentation comes off Nell
and I went it was very interesting indeed it was grand vincent ever
constant

WEDNESDAY, NOVEMBER 18, 1863.

came hom with us Cristy was chairman for the evening he did not see
us very busy today hannah brown Celestine and Sally Mathers and
nelly was up here this evening

THURSDAY 19

we had quite a lovely time quite pleasant i was busy home fixing up
my things part of the afternoon Nell and i went to Mary Jane heard
many cheering[77] [. . .]

FRIDAY 20

mr Lively has promised to teach our school we expect to comence
next Monday night tom sails tomorrow I stoped home a little while

SATURDAY, NOVEMBER 21, 1863.

very rainy day Nelly did not get up to day Mr Powel has bin quite
generous to day i have bin woching the weather all the evening in
hopes it stop raining so I could go home

SUNDAY 22

liz Brown was here last night very pleasent day I went to church in
the afternoon very good sermon after church i went to Joneses Bible
class at his mrs [. . .]

MONDAY 23

I have been quite sick all day my throat[78] has not got well yet
i anticipat a great deal of pleasure this evening Nell [. . .] mills and i
went down to school

77. The cheering Emilie reports may
have originated from Philadelphians
celebrating news of Lincoln's Gettysburg
Address, presented earlier that day one
hundred miles west of Philadelphia.
Articles concerning the address were
printed the next morning in Philadelphia's
newspapers. "The 'Gettysburg' Celebration. Our Great National Cemetery,"
Philadelphia Inquirer, November 20, 1863.

78. On December 19, Emilie visited
a doctor about her sore throat, but she

TUESDAY, NOVEMBER 24, 1863.

we had a very nice school Mr. Lively could not stay we comence
next monday night quite a disagreeable day in the evening I went to
meeting very good

WEDNESDAY 25

meeting nothing of intrest happened to day i have not bin out for
a wander I have bin expecting Nellie but she did not come bernice
stoped her

THURSDAY 26

this evening left a not for john Simson today is Thanksgiving day
i went to church in the afternoon after church I went with liz to call
on rachel turner

FRIDAY, NOVEMBER 27, 1863.

i spent the [. . .] Nellie quite dull to what last Thanksgiving[79] was
many changes since then yesterday one year ago Mary was up here
but she has gone to rest I hope

SATURDAY 28

very rainy day Nell did not get up here very busey all day in the
evening I stoped home and at Nellies Frank is still at EJs

SUNDAY 29

very dull morning I went to church heard quite a good sermon [. . .]
out Bible class at Whites very good turn out Mr bustil[80] came home
with me Cristy

---

continued to suffer from the ailment until
December 31. The *Recorder* advertised a
variety of treatments for sore throat. Such
products included "Browns' Bronchial Tro-
ches," salt treatments, Wistar's Balsam of
Wild Cherry, Wishart's Pine Tree Tar Cor-
dial, and Wilsonia Magnetic insoles (meant
to prevent "cold feet," which the article
suggested often caused a sore throat). The
Recorder and other local newspapers, such
as the *Village Record*, also noted many

individuals who died from illnesses such as
a "malignant sore throat" and an outbreak
of "putrid sore throat" during the 1860s.
In light of this, it is perhaps unsurprising
that Emilie would consult a doctor.

79. Thanksgiving must have been
a somber affair for Emilie, after Mary's
death, Alfred's departure, and the prospect of EJ's being drafted.

80. The Bustill family was prominent
in Philadelphia. The "Mr. Bustill" who

MONDAY, NOVEMBER 30, 1863.

went with with Mary Clay very cold Nell was up here in the after
noon we went down to school found Mr lively waiting for us hannah

TUESDAY, DECEMBER 1

brown was there P meeting at Mrs turners after meeting we stoped at
bustils had quite a Pleasant chat

WEDNESDAY 2

Cristy still Teaching i do not know how to treat him i certainly do not
feel the same towards him nell was up this evening

THURSDAY, DECEMBER 3, 1863.

Thursday very Pleasent Nell Mrs Jordan and i went out shoping nell
bought herself a coat we went up to harrises then paid several other
visits

FRIDAY 4

in the evening we went to hear Fred Duglass[81] yesterday I Paid a visit
to the White house[82] i have bin so busy i have not had time to write

---

accompanied Emilie home might have
been George Bustill White, who was
thirty years old in 1863. See the entries for
Charles Bustill and George Bustill White
in the list of people and institutions in the
front matter of this volume. 1860 United
States Federal Census, Philadelphia
Ward 13, Philadelphia, Pennsylvania, roll
M653_1163, page 682, image 268, family
history library film 805163; Silcox, "Philadelphia Negro Educator," 88–89.

81. To commemorate its own
thirtieth anniversary, the American
Anti-Slavery Society held a convention in
Philadelphia's Concert Hall. William Lloyd
Garrison presided, and Lucretia Mott was
a featured speaker. Abolitionist luminaries
such as Owen Lovejoy and Charles
Sumner sent letters attacking slavery
and discussing impending Congressional

action on abolition. Frederick Douglass
was a keynote speaker in the evening
session on December 4. "City Affairs,"
North American and United States Gazette
(Philadelphia), December 4, 1863;
"The Abolition Convention. Meeting of a
Mutual Admiration Club. Semi-Feminine
Men and Strong-Minded Women," *Daily
Age*, December 4, 1863.

82. George Bustill White had six siblings, all listed as living at home in 1860;
see the list of people and institutions in
the front matter of this volume. It is not
difficult to imagine the White household's
being the center of much activity during
and after the Civil War. 1860 United
States Federal Census, Philadelphia Ward
12 Division 1, Philadelphia, Pennsylvania,
roll M653_1162, page 125, image 129,
family history library film 805162.

FIGURE 12   Lucretia Mott. Lucretia Mott was among the speakers at the thirtieth anniversary celebration of the American Anti-Slavery Society. Philadelphia's Camp William Penn was located adjacent to Lucretia Mott's home, which for years had served as a gathering place for black and white abolitionists, fugitive slaves, and suffragists. Photo courtesy of the Library of Congress.

SATURDAY 5

very clear we have not had a clear Saturday for some time i was down town a little while

SUNDAY, DECEMBER 6, 1863.

to is a very interesting to all Chrristians it is our inter communion St mary [. . .] communed with us Bible class at whites good number out

MONDAY 7

quite cold out Nell was up here this afternoon we went down to school we have quite a dull school not organized and appointed a committe

TUESDAY 8

to elect officers meeting at Mernick sons after meeting we went to bustils as usual meeting is there next time

WEDNESDAY, DECEMBER 9, 1863.

very busy cleaning house every thing upside down last night I saw sony taylor and heard tomy amos was here i hope i will get

THURSDAY 10

to see him I have bin trying to collect money for the organ[83] tom was at EJs this evening he went down to mrs hills with nell and i we spent quite

FRIDAY 11

a Pleasent evening dane Chester was there and vincent Nell was up here and by norristown come up in the evening the

SATURDAY, DECEMBER 12, 1863.

is quite lively very dull day i have bin very busey began to get my Dress done tom was up and went down home a little

---

83. Emilie's efforts to collect money for an "organ" may have been for the Anti-Slavery Society or another abolitionist organization. Frederick Douglass spoke again on Thursday, December 10, about the war, abolition, and suffrage for African Americans. "City Intelligence," *Philadelphia Inquirer*, December 12, 1863.

SUNDAY 13

while raining i went to church hardly any ones out Doct Jones
Preached he gave us an exelent sermon Nell was up

MONDAY 14

in the evening i went Down to school this evening very [. . .] out
Nell and i spent the school

TUESDAY, DECEMBER 15, 1863.

meeting at bustills i am sory to say i was very Drowsey after meeting
we staid a little while Cristy and Virgil came in we soon went after

WEDNESDAY 16

they came in and to our surprise Cristy came up home with us Nell
came up this evening Tom was not here i was very busy trying to get

THURSDAY 17

my Dress done raing all day i went hom quite late Sarah was busy
Mr gibbs was to lecture to night tom went home

FRIDAY, DECEMBER 18, 1863

with me i got my dress greased last night but i got it out to day tomy
was up a little while to night

SATURDAY 19

very busey to day i went up to the Docts to consult him about my
Throat stoped home nell has made her bonnet

SUNDAY 20

very cold i was not out in the morning we had a stranger Preach in
the afternoon in the evening while class

MONDAY, DECEMBER 21, 1863.

at stills very few out I hav sick all day i went down to school it was
quite cold there I cought more cold very few girls down Plenty

TUESDAY 22

of gentlemen i have bin quite sick all day not able to go to meeting

WEDNESDAY 23

Sue was here this morning i could hardly talk to her Nelly has not bin up here since monday

THURSDAY, DECEMBER 24, 1863.

very cold today Sue was here and brought our ribbion i went down home very Dull Christmas eve[84] I felt so sick i have to go home

FRIDAY 25

soon very fine day but i could not enJoy myself i had such a cold Nellie and i went to bustill and had som egg nog we met Cristy he went

SATURDAY 26

around to aunt Janes with us i had to go hom i spent a [. . .] time vincent and Nell came up and staid a little While with me

SUNDAY, DECEMBER 27, 1863.

raining all day i did not get to church all day lizzie was sick Nell and liz came up after church we spent the evening rather dull vincent did not come

MONDAY 28

up raining all day lizzie sick to day i have not bin home since Friday I did not go to school on acount of the weather Nell was

TUESDAY 29

down cloudy to day Sue was here this morning EJ stoped in this afternoon i did not get to meeting i am sorry to say i was home

WEDNESDAY, DECEMBER 30, 1863.

nice clear morning after the rain very busy all day Nellie was up here spent the evening vincent was up and staid a little

THURSDAY 31

while clear and [. . .] cold i have bin quite sick all the week Nell and Tomy was up here Nell and went out a little while stoped in to

---

84. Emilie elaborates on her holiday activities in the memoranda pages at the end of her 1863 diary.

bustills then went up to teach first er and helped trim the childrens
tree stoped at mrs hills sue went withes us to aunt Janes i was

Memoranda.

I sent two letters up to harrisburg by harriet Chester I have one dollar
of [. . .] I have written two letters to my sister and have received no
answer Addel gordon called to see me and
Friday last 20 i owe her a visit the first Sunday in every month i must
cut the ends of my hair
The Baneker gurds started for Harrisburge on the 17th returned on the
18th without a scare[85]

Memoranda.

Wednsday the 17th 1863 will be rememberd by a great many of our
People nearly all of our best young men left for the war but happily
returned the next day un harmed
Sarah Thomas was married on last Saturday the 20th of June
Monday the 29th the most exciting day ever witness by having
Refugees[86] line the streets from all the towns this side of

Memoranda.

Harrisburg and even from Harrisburg
The riot[87] in New York comenced on Monday the 13th contnued over
five days the Colored People suffrd most from the mob

---

85.   After the December 31, 1863, entry,
Emilie filled up pages titled "Memoranda"
with various news items, social obligations,
reminders, and to-do lists. She seems
also to have used these pages as a place
to record some of the most memorable
moments of 1863, like her description
of Governor Andrew Curtin's refusal to
accept black recruits to defend the state
from Lee's invasion in June 1863 and the
refugees from south-central Pennsylvania
who fled the Army of Northern Virginia.

86.   Residents of south-central Pennsylvania fled the advancing Confederate

troops. Emilie also notes this event
on June 29, 1863. Harrold, *Border War*,
209–10.

87.   More than one hundred people,
mostly African Americans, were killed in
New York City's draft riots from July 13
to 16, 1863. Many more left the city afterward. Philadelphia avoided the serious
draft resistance that New York experienced, largely because, one suspects, the
city took on the appearance of a military
camp, with so many troops making their
way to and from Washington. Gallman,
Mastering Wartime, 34.

Wednsday the 5 will allways remember some and while i was over
Jersey opened my trunk and stoled a ring and $6.00 and 74 cents in
silver
I sent alfred his notice on the 10th of august

Memoranda.
I had two letters from Nellie in two weeks only one from EJ
Georgeana has bin married about three weekes her husband beat
her and left the other day she had to go back to be uncles the honey
moon is not over
Em Jones has bin married nearly a week i hope she will make out
beter than poor Gorgana Rowley has disgraced her shamfuly

Memoranda.
I spent a very dull Christmas this year i was sick Christmas eve and had
to go home New years eve i was out a little while it rained so hard i did
get any where i stoped at bustels Cristye was there as usaly Nell went
to Miss Sicos Party Sue was up here in the morning John cam after her

Memoranda.
Oh if i had a kind friend
A friend that i could trust
Twould be a source of joy to me
To know that i was [. . .]
With one in whom i could confide
My secrets hopes and fears
and who would not in coldness turn
From me in future years
But oh i fear i never shall
Have that consoling thought
To help me on through lifes
cold storm
Tough [Though] very close ive sought
To find this Jewel of a friend
That Poets so applaud
And as i have not found one yet
I fear it's all a fraud

1 8 6 4

JANUARY, FRIDAY, 1, 1864.

I feel Thankful that i am spard to see a nother year home all day in the evening i went to James i enjoyed myself very much great many changes have taken place since last new year

SATURDAY, 2.

I staid home last night bitter cold day i stoped in to see Nell Poor girl she is very un happy Sue was here to day and two strong ladies from boston i came out and bought my diary to day

SUNDAY, 3.

very cold this morning I was not at church in the morning i feel thankful that i have bin spared to see the first Sabbath in the new year very good attendance in the afternoon I was doen no bible class It was quite a dis appointment Nell and I went to church

JANUARY, MONDAY, 4, 1864.

very cold it comenced snowing this morning before [. . .] we had quite a snow storm sue was up and staid until school time I went down to school had a very nice school but we had no fire i had to hurry home soon[1]

1. Snow storms started in the Midwest on New Year's Eve and swept eastward, disrupting train travel and delaying the movement of troops in the Shenandoah Valley. The papers reported on weather-related fatalities from Chicago to New York. The intense cold that followed the storms claimed additional victims. "Army of the Potomac," *Philadelphia Inquirer*, January 1, 1864, 3; "Important from West Virginia—The Rebel Raid a Complete Failure," *Illustrated New Age* (Philadelphia), January 8, 1864, 2.

TUESDAY, 5.

quite cold to day I was out a little [. . .] went tom Sunday I went to see Em warwich then out to see Lizzie meeting to night at rachels after [. . .]ing we went to [. . .] bustil than to the fair[2]

WEDNESDAY, 6.

staid at nells all night vincent came here with me i do not know how i could get along with out him Nell and sue were both here to day they are going to spend the evening with the girls

JANUARY, THURSDAY, 7, 1864.

quite cold to day sue was up to day I went out to harrises then to see lizzie then over to Sarah Whites it was six oclock before i got home in the evening we went to the fair had quite a nice

FRIDAY, 8.

time vincent came home with us cristy was there and acted quite strangely Nell was up to day i fell so sorry for her Tomy made me a present last night I was up to see hannah brown sue has not bin here to day

SATURDAY, 9.

Bitter cold to day very busy all day mrs Cisco came up in the afternoon i went with her to get a clock in the evening i went down home I brought my gration up

JANUARY, SUNDAY, 10, 1864.

very cold i went Down to church one of mr gibbes friends Preached a very good Sermon i expected Sue up here but she did not get here i spent quite a lonsome evening all by my self

2. On January 5 and continuing until January 7, 1864, the LUA hosted a fair to raise money in support of its efforts to provide for sick and wounded USCT soldiers convalescing in and around Philadelphia. The *Recorder* advertised the event at the Sansom Street Hall and asked that "the friends of the soldier every where attend." "Soldier's Fair," *Christian Recorder*, January 7, 1864.

MONDAY, 11.

quite cold but clear Nellie was up in the afternoon sue spent the
evening with her i went down to schoole stoped at mrs hills and
mrs Hawkins Paid up my dreas we had a

TUESDAY, 12.

very nice School we elected three offices Gorge Jhon and Nell meeting
mr whrigites very Spirited meeting lizzie was up and staid untill
meeting time Nell did not go

JANUARY, WEDNESDAY, 13, 1864.

very busy to day i have bin waiting Patiently for nell to come up
this evening but she did not come she went to Milley to a membing
Presentation

THURSDAY, 14.

very Disagreeable to day the walking is very had [hard] I went down
to the conn[. . .]ation office and hills spent Part of the evening in
home and the rest

FRIDAY, 15.

of the evening in nells sue came up and Spent Part of the day and
evening Nell was sick i sent a letter to Will yesterday

JANUARY, SATURDAY, 16, 1864.

Elwood was quite Sick Thursday Nell stoped an her my [. . .]
to monls i was down home stoped in mills

SUNDAY, 17.

very Disagreeable evening i was not at our church all day it [. . .]
inter communion at st marys Nell was sick liz and went great meeting
at bethel bible class

MONDAY, 18.

at Mary Jones very nice class raining hard all day Nell stoped for me
to go to school but i did not go on account of the rain

JANUARY, TUESDAY, 19, 1864.

Still raining i wrote a letter to Sister on Sunday meeting at Depees very few out mr gibbs was not there [. . .] still quite sick Nell did not go to meeting

WEDNESDAY, 20.

sue stoped here a minute beutiful day after the rain Nell came up to spend the evening she has recived her little badget of affection sue and John

THURSDAY, 21.

stoped in a little while Nell is up here ironing i went out to Mary Cloyes she was not home Called on [. . .] she was out spent the rest of the day home in the evening we went to the lecture

JANUARY, FRIDAY, 22, 1864.

Mr Stonford lectured his subject was the fire of moloch lovely day i was down home and stoped for nell to come up and made a finish i was down to bustil a few minutes

SATURDAY, 23.

very busy all day today was up in the morning and brought Nells guiatar I went down home [. . .] was very sick Sarah is quite worried about him

SUNDAY, 24.

very dull day Nell was not at church this morning She was sick Elwood was very ill this morning Elijah and Sarah are very ansoius about him Sue and John and Nell and vincent

JANUARY, MONDAY, 25, 1864.

were up to see me in the evening we spent quite a Pleasant evening Fine day Elwood is still very sick I went down to school had a very full school Miss little was down I staid home

TUESDAY, 26.

all night with buh he is very low the fever has gone to his head Poor little fellow he suffers very much meeting at bustils i could not go Elwood has not spoken since this mor

WEDNESDAY, 27.

ning [morning] i staid with him him all night last night lizzie came home to day Rachel goes to this evening i spent Part of the evening home Elwood is not better Mary B and mother

JANUARY, THURSDAY, 28, 1864.

attend to him faithfully i went to see mrs newhall and to send somethings out to Frank Elizah has call in Doct [. . .] Morris but i [. . .] it is to late for any earthly Power to help him

FRIDAY, 29.

i staid down home last night [. . .] is sinking fast to day i was to go over to see Frank but i cant go Elwood if still suffering but i think Death will be a good end his suffering

SATURDAY, 30.

Tomy came to me this morning Elwood is diing I hurried home and staid untill he breathed his last he died[3] at 11 o clock this evening his spirit has gon to his father that quiet

JANUARY, SUNDAY, 31, 1864.

very gloomy day i went down home and staid untill after ten the girls all stoped to see me there was a great many People in to see Sarah and EJ i [. . .] wrote to Alfred this evening

FEBRUARY, MONDAY, 1.

very rainy all day Nell was up we went for our guitars[4] i did not go down to school sue was down they had quite a nice time

3. Elwood's death certificate confirms the four-year-old boy's death on January 30, 1864, of "congestion of the brain." Little Elwood's death must have hit the family particularly hard. "Pennsylvania, Philadelphia City Death Certificates, 1803–1915," index and images, FamilySearch, https://familysearch.org/pal:/MM9.1.1/JF89-RY1 (accessed May 8, 2013), Elwood O. Davis, 1864.

4. On November 13, 1863, Emilie writes of receiving guitar strings from Tomy.

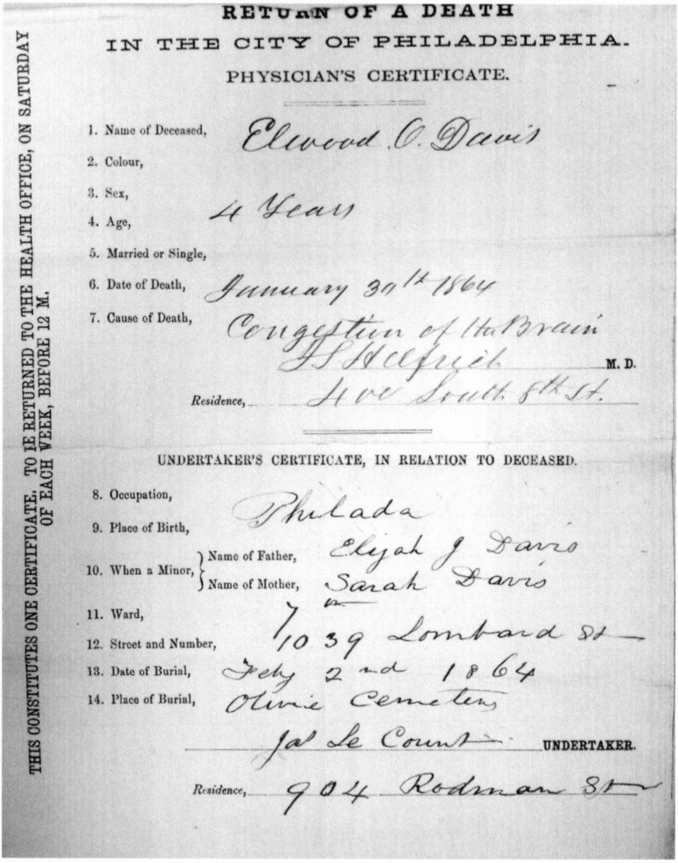

FIGURE 13 Elwood Davis's death certificate. Elijah and Sarah Davis's son, four-year-old Elwood, died on January 30, 1864. Elwood Davis, Return of Death, burial date: February 2, 1864, Olive Cemetery. Courtesy of Philadelphia City Archives.

TUESDAY, 2.

quite dull this morning this is the day we have to Part with our little Elwood i went down home in the morning Mrs williams laid him out very nice but he did not look like himself mr gibbs spoke beutifuly

FEBRUARY, WEDNESDAY, 3, 1864.

[. . .] over him i staid home all the afternoon i did not go up to hzards untill 10 i went down to bustills with hannah sue came in to had her head Dressed very fine day Nell came up this evening and hannah Brown

THURSDAY, 4.

I got my gutair yesterday i went went up to augustins with Sue then down to bustills i spent the evening at bustills i received a letter from tom and one from his friend vincent came home with

FRIDAY, 5.

me mr gibbs has a daughter egerton is sick he looks badly I have bin waiting for nell to come up all day but she has not made her appearance as yet this evening sue stoped on her way to

FEBRUARY, SATURDAY, 6, 1864.

meeting very dull and rainy i have not bin well all day i went down home a little while and stoped in to nells

SUNDAY, 7.

very dull all day great many out in the afternoon mr gibbs Preached a sermon concerning the several death wich has occured in our church during the past month

MONDAY, 8.

beautiful day i went down chestnut st this afternoon meet neal miller I went down [. . .] to school in the evening we had a very hard lesson we Practiced several peiceis for wednesday evening

FEBRUARY, TUESDAY, 9, 1864.

Sue stoped here this morning quite busy all day i sent a letter to tom yesterday meeting at offerts liz and i went nell did not go we had a very good meeting few out

WEDNESDAY, 10.

quite today mrs rock is to buried this morning Jenie and i went up
Chesnut St to see the colored soldiers[5] they went away to day in the
evening we went to Madame [. . .] in read

THURSDAY, 11.

she well quite a good house Dave was down i went up to lives this
afternoon Stoped home went on erand for EJ then went down to
bustils Spent Part of the evening there and the

FEBRUARY, FRIDAY, 12, 1864.

after Part at nels sue come up and spent the day John come up in the
evening Nellie was up a little while i have not bin out to day John and
Sue had French on

SATURDAY, 13.

quite Pleasent i intend up to Storing in the home this evening but nell
comame up here [. . .] and brought here gutare and for me to take
dow i did not go home

SUNDAY, 14.

quite a blustry day i did not go out in the morning we had a very
good sermon bible class at nellies great many there i had to march
home

FEBRUARY, MONDAY, 15, 1864.

quite cold but clear i went down to school we had a very full school
mr lively divided the classes i Stoped at Doct helfriches tomy is quite
sick

---

5.   On Wednesday, February 10, the
22nd Infantry Regiment of the USCT
marched from Camp William Penn
through the streets of Philadelphia on
their way south, where they would see
action at Yorktown and Petersburg and
later occupy Richmond. The *Recorder*
reported that at the head of "1,000 strong,
with bayonets gleaming and glittering in
the sun," rode their commanding officer,
Lieutenant Colonel Louis Wagner, and
the commander who would lead them
into the field, Colonel Joseph Kiddoo. The
Recorder noted that "they were the theme
of general admiration and applause," and
it disparaged the cowardice of the few who
insulted the troops: "How many of them
would be willing to shoulder the musket
in the negro's stead?" "The 22d," *Christian
Recorder*, February 13, 1864.

TUESDAY, 16.

quite windy to day meeting at mrs harmons very few out only the
Nellie [. . .] and liz and i and mr white weights the meetings are very
poorly attended

WEDNESDAY, 17.

Bitter cold day the coldest this winter i had to go out very much
against my will Sue has not bin up this week

FEBRUARY, THURSDAY, 18, 1864

still quite cold To day is my birthday i went home then to mr livelys
he was not home I feel Thanful that i have bin spared to see another
birthday vincent came up

FRIDAY, 19.

Here to treat me it was almost eleven o clock tom is still sick Nellie
and i spent last evening in signours mary plaed severl peices for us

SATURDAY, 20.

very Pleasent to day busy all day as usal in evening i went down
home Nell was up in the afternoon Sue was here in the morning She
has gone to Chester to spend a copel of days

FEBRUARY, SUNDAY, 21, 1864.

lovely morning i went down to church Nell was not out more but
liz and i after church we went to see aunty hollis stoped in bustels a
minute vincent was up to see me this afternoon

MONDAY, 22.

to is very fine there is to be a grand parade pass our house [. . .]
to day in the after noon Magdalline Scott and lizzie agresstes stoped
to see me in the evening i went down to school we had

TUESDAY, 23.

a nice time to day i have bin sick all day i did not go to meeting i gone
not seen nell since last night meeting was at [. . .] Mary Block is quite
sick

FEBRUARY, WEDNESDAY, 24, 1864.

busy as usal to day Sue come up from Chester this morning She is
quite sick with a bad cold She was here most all the morning Nellie
did not come up i was quite Disappointed

THURSDAY, 25.

quite pleasent to day I went down to mr Livelys but did not take a
lesson[6] i was out collecting this afternoon but did not rase a cent in
the evening nell and i went to bustels

FRIDAY, 26.

quite dull to day Nell was up

FEBRUARY, SATURDAY, 27, 1864.

busy as usal nell stoped up this morning in the eveing Phine and i
when down home and Stoped at nells we went up eleventh St and
saw a [. . .] sight

SUNDAY, 28.

Pleasent i went to church in the afternoon heard an exelent sermon
after church liz and i went to bustels and spent quite a Pleasant time
in the evening we went to bible class at adyees

MONDAY, 29.

nell and lizz i went down to mr livelys and stoped at mr Potters
we had a very nice schooll great many out we have two classes now
vincent went home with me

MARCH, TUESDAY, 1, 1864.

very stormy all day snowing fast all day meeting at Mis Mills very
few out but we had a good meeting

WEDNESDAY, 2.

nell did not come up as usal we went to her Place this morning i hop
she will like it

6. Emilie takes lessons from
Mr. Lively approximately every Monday
and Thursday until June 2, 1864. However,
she does not mention specifically what
kind of lessons she was taking.

THURSDAY, 3.

very Pleasent [. . .] head i went to 20 and Chesnut st looking for neal
but did not find him i stoped in [. . .] then went to mrs Crist [. . .]

MARCH, FRIDAY, 4, 1864.

Pleasent to day lizzie holms stoped in to see me

SATURDAY, 5.

raining to day very busy all day i did not go home Nell stoped this
morning

SUNDAY, 6.

beutiful morning i went to church in the morning communion in
the after noon i am sorry to say i was not out in the afternoon in the
evening Sue and nell came

MARCH, MONDAY, 7, 1864.

up John and gorge and spent the evening I went down to school
this evening went to mr Livelys first we had a very nice school quite
pleasant

TUESDAY, 8.

to day meeting this evening at mrs Browns we had quite a showing
mr benadict died Suddenly this afternoon he was at church on last
Sunday morning

WEDNESDAY, 9.

mr Brown is quite sick Sue and little girl was here to day it seems an
age since nell has bin up here on wednesday evening

MARCH, THURSDAY, 10, 1864.

quite a disagreable day I went out shoping and got a Pair of armlets
for the minesters dress i stoped home a while then Nellie and I went
down

FRIDAY, 11.

Nell did not go in i went in and spent quite an agreable time then
went to aunt Janes and took tea Baker came up home with us

SATURDAY, 12.

I went down home a little while Nell was not very well I came home and comenced Practicing

MARCH, SUNDAY, 13, 1864.

very Pleasant to day i did not go out i wrote Three letters in the morning In the after noon I went to church and heard a very good sermon in the evening

MONDAY, 14.

to bible class at Mrs riders Nell did not go lizzie stoped this evening to go school i had to leave her and go to mr lively we had quite a number out mr lively

TUESDAY, 15.

was not there i came out before school was out meeting at mr stewards great many we had real old time Prayer meeting mrs Thomas was there

MARCH, WEDNESDAY, 16, 1864

very busy all day i expected Nellie in the evening but as usal she did not come I received a letter from Martin yesterday

THURSDAY, 17.

lovely day I went up to harrises lizzie Fe wa quite sick i stoped to see Sue a little while Nell and went to Mr Welles then to mrs oneils and Brown we spent the evening

FRIDAY, 18.

With Sue mrs hill gave me the childrens Pothographs quite busy to Sue stoped in a few minutes yesterday i stoped at Mrs butters on

MARCH, SATURDAY, 19, 1864.

Put my name for a situation[7] Nellie was out to come up a little while this evening i went down home and cut out a dress for Mrs Burton

7. Here, "situation" likely refers to work as a domestic.

SUNDAY, 20.

quite raw and cold to day I went down to church in the morning very
good sermon after church we went to see som sick members liz and i
stoped at Mr gibbs in the evening the girls came up vincent

MONDAY, 21.

John and Barker we spent quite an agreeable time quite cold i went
to mr livelys as usal then to school we had quite a nice school Barker
was down Peterson and Baker came home with me

MARCH, TUESDAY, 22, 1864.

very chilly and cold she stoped here to day her and Jain spating again
meeting at our house we had a very happy meeting EJ was out Sarah
did not come up

WEDNESDAY, 23.

quite a snow storm it snowed all night very disagreeable out Sue ran
in a minute there was a funeral down at the church this afternoon
a stranger i did

THURSDAY, 24.

not get down very fine day i did not go out untill late not Living
Well I went down to See Mrs newhall stoped to see Mrs Brown
Stoped at [. . .] spent the evening with Nellie

MARCH, FRIDAY, 25, 1864.

Sue stoped a little Nell was up i expectd Barker but it comenced
raining and he did not com I was quite disapoited but i was so busy
sewing i had to forget it

SATURDAY, 26.

raining and very disagreeable all day i finished my dress and took
[. . .] it home they scolded me at home for coming out in the storm

SUNDAY, 27.

lovely day after the rain this is easter Sunday it ought to be solemnly
observed i went to church in the afternoon heard a very good sermon
in the evening i went to bible class we had an

MARCH, MONDAY, 28, 1864.

very interesting class it was at [. . .] quite Pleasent to day i went to
Mr Livelys had a very nice lesson then went down to school Sue and
vincent went to the fair[8]

TUESDAY, 29.

i went down home and fitted sarahs dress then went to meeting had a
very nice meting after meeting Mary and i went to the fair it was very
nice

WEDNESDAY, 30.

quite disagreeable all day raining barker came up and spent the
evening with me we had quite a nice little chat Nell and [. . .] wister
stoped on their way

MARCH, THURSDAY, 31, 1864.

to the fair very dull to day i went down to Mr Liveleys having my
lesson in the afternoon i went home and sewed Nell came for me to
go out she bout her Piecs and we paid two

APRIL, FRIDAY, 1.

visits in the evening we went to the fair i enjoyed myself very much
i had several Presents given to me Nell [. . .] at the to night i did not go

SATURDAY 2.

another rainy Saturday i have not seen the girls since Thursday neale
and nell stoped for me to go to the fair there was love Presentations a
[. . .] To conel [colonel] wagner[9]

8. The LUA hosted a weeklong fair
for the benefit of sick and wounded USCT
soldiers at the Concert Hall beginning
on March 28. Emilie writes in her diary
of attending this particular fair on three
separate days and notes rainy weather
on the three days she did not attend the
fair. The *Recorder* reported that the fair
raised $1,032.84, though the poor weather
lowered attendance, leaving "about three
hundred dollars worth of goods unsold."
The article notes that the LUA donated
$200 of the proceeds to the Penn Relief
Association "for the benefit of the sick and
wounded colored soldiers." "The Ladies'
Fair, Held in Concert Hall, for Soldiers,"
Christian Recorder, April 30, 1864.

9. Wounded at the second battle
of Bull Run, Lieutenant Colonel Louis
Wagner became commanding officer
at Camp William Penn, where he was
instrumental in recruiting and preparing
black soldiers and white officers for
service to the U.S. Army. After the war,

FIGURE 14 Lieutenant Colonel Louis Wagner. Louis Wagner (middle, seated) served as commanding officer of Camp William Penn. Germantown Historical Society, Philadelphia, Pennsylvania.

APRIL, SUNDAY, 3, 1864.

in rather cloudy and damp i went to church herd a very good
exortation from one of the many men at the college we went to
bethel after church nell was not out in the evening sue and nell John
and vincent and barker

MONDAY, 4.

come up we spent quite an agreeable evening barker goes away
to day cloudy to day I went to mr livelys and taken my lesson then
went down to schooll he was not there vincent was not there

TUESDAY, 5.

we had quite a full school very stormy to day it has bin raining
hailing and snowing[10] mrs Beck leaft for [. . .] this morning quite a
sorrowfull time the rain Prevented me from going to Meeting

APRIL, WEDNESDAY, 6, 1864.

lovely day i have bin quite busy all day as usal in the afternoon i went
out of an erand stoped home a minute found a letter there from mary
Williams with her Potograph enclosed it was

THURSDAY, 7.

quite a joyfull suprprise beutiful morning i went down to Mr Livelys
but did not take my lesson my finger to raw Mr lively advised me not
to I went around to see Mrs bridge and stoped at aunt Janes Sue and

FRIDAY, 8.

went out shoping Mary holack and i went to see Poor Mr fairbanx
he was hurt by the explosion[11] on Wednsday he looks very badly
to day i have not bin out sarah sent me word

Wagner served as the Pennsylvania state
commander of the Grand Army of the
Republic, an organization open to white
and black veterans and, according to
historian Andrew Tremel, "expressed an
appreciation of black military contribu-
tions." Bacon, *But One Race*, 149; Tremel,
"The Union League," 15, 27.

10. This appears to have been an
abnormal series of rainstorms for the East
Coast. On April 6, the *Inquirer* reported
that the "rain storm continues without
intermission." "Effects of the Storm,"
Philadelphia Inquirer, April 6, 1864.

11. An article in the *Daily Age* on
April 7, titled "Terrific Boiler Explosion,"

APRIL, SATURDAY, 9, 1864.

yesterday that Charles Signour was dead it does seem that death is in the land both amoung young and old very [. . .] this morning it [. . .] a raining before dark i will not get home to night

SUNDAY, 10.

quite a rainy morning i did not go to church in the morning i went out in the afternoon Nellie was not out her finger still quite bad bible class with Mrs Williams very few

MONDAY, 11.

out beautiful day i went to see Charly he was buried to day i went down to Mr livelys then to school and collected $3.0 towards paying the debt

APRIL, TUESDAY, 12, 1864.

on the organ meeting at Mrs Chases Sunrise was there and spoke beautiful we had a very good meeting Mrs brown is still very ill

WEDNESDAY, 13.

an other rainy day i have bin busy as usal Nell did not get up the soldiers were to Proder to day but was posponed on account of the rain[12]

---

described a devastating blast caused by an exploding boiler at the Merrick & Sons Foundry, located between Fourth and Fifth Streets and Washington and Federal Streets in Philadelphia. The windows of nearly all the buildings in the area were blown out by the shock wave. Seven workers were killed in the blast, and a number of others were injured, including Jacob Farbeaux, a member of Emilie's church and occasional preacher, listed by the *Daily Age* as having suffered a broken arm and fractured skull. Born around 1801 in South Carolina, Jacob Farbeaux died on December 26, 1874. His death certificate lists his occupation as "Messenger to Merrick & Co," matching the *Daily Age* article's

description of him as "colored, messenger." "Pennsylvania, Philadelphia City Death Certificates, 1803–1915," index and images, FamilySearch, https://familysearch.org/pal:/MM9.1.1/JK3L-ZNP (accessed May 8, 2013), Jacob Farbeaux, 1874.

12. The parade of the USCT stationed at Camp William Penn, including five companies of the 25th Regiment, 32nd Regiment, and six companies of the 43rd Regiment, was scheduled to take place on April 13 but was postponed until the following day, when soldiers marched through Philadelphia. After the parade, the troops were entertained at the refreshment saloons. "Parade of Colored Troops," *Philadelphia Inquirer*, April 15, 1864.

THURSDAY, 14.

quite an [. . .] to day i went down to mr livelys as usal the Soldier
Parade to day i saw them at center and Wattem Nell Lizzie and i went
down to eigth and lombard and saw

APRIL, FRIDAY, 15, 1864.

them in their glory it seemed to be a free day beutiful morning i went
out of errnd stoped at lizes and bustels J B had quite a Promanade[13]

SATURDAY, 16.

clear for the first in three weeks but comenced to rain before my EJ
i went and left my bonnets stoped down and allow kate and Sue were
here

SUNDAY, 17

lovely morning i went to church Mr Sunrise Preached for us he gone
on the Plain Doctrine in the evening Sue came up Nell did not come
vincent and John came up [. . .]

APRIL, MONDAY, 18, 1864.

beautiful day quite like spring [. . .] the Wedding is expected I went
down to Mr livelys had a very good lesson then went down in to the
schooll i had to open the school and light up

TUESDAY, 19.

another beutiful day Sue was here she was not down to school last
night meeting at Mr Wells very good meeting Poor Nellie had to go
home her finger Pained her so i went up to the

WEDNESDAY, 20.

depot but was to late the folks had come i was so disaponted they
are stoping at hardings Nell was up this evening she has not been for
some time before her finger is better

13.   Black Philadelphians showed their
support by attending parades of USCT
soldiers who trained at Camp William

Penn. Wert, "Camp William Penn," 335,
340–42.

APRIL, THURSDAY, 21, 1864.

lovely day i went down to Mr livelys had a nice lesson in the
afternoon i went up and sit for [. . .] some potographs [photographs]
then went down to call on the suide they had gone out

FRIDAY, 22.

went back home and found them two i went with them to pay off
some calls i taken tea with them and spent the evening with them
we had a grand time Nell and Sue did not

SATURDAY, 23.

like it i went up to the depot gathering but they did not go in till
half past 10 at night hall received some handsome presents They all
looked lovely nell was up this evening i got a pair of

APRIL, SUNDAY, 24, 1864.

garters this is a lovely Sabbath morning i would like to go to church
this morning I went in the afternoon Sunrise spoke for us bible class
at Mrs hills i heard some very bad news to day

MONDAY, 25.

yesterday i wrote to Mary Williams i went for my potographs they
were not very good i sent one to Mary Williams gone and to Mrs hill
i went to Mr livelys as usal then to school

TUESDAY, 26.

we had a very wise school meeting at Mr whites very few out lizzie
gave me one of her Pictures to day my album is all most full

APRIL, WEDNESDAY, 27, 1864.

rainy day busy as usal Sue was here but I did not see her Nell came
up and spent the evening with me she was trying to sew in [. . .] her
hand band

THURSDAY, 28.

i am so busy i can not help her fine day i went up to mr [. . .] stoped
at Nate's I heard of a situation to go to germantown for the summer
Nell and I were out sh

FRIDAY, 29.

oping [shopping] i spent the evening with Mary and Nell Neal was
there Sue was not down i have not seen her since monay home all
day Neal Promised to come over to night but

APRIL, SATURDAY, 30, 1864.

did not lovely day i went out to germantown to Mrs Wister[14] and
engageed to go to her the first of June i did not get [. . .] to is the last
of April

SUNDAY, 1.

rather cloudy this morning i went to church we had a stranger to
speak for us after church we went to bethel Sue Nell and John and
Gorge were up in the evening

MONDAY, 2.

beautiful day busy as usal on mondays in the evening i went to
mr livelys I did not know my lesson very well i went down to scholl
had a very nice school vincent

MAY, TUESDAY, 3, 1864.

was not there it being the first monday in the month quite warm
to day i went down home and received my circular for the
exsominotion[15] meeting at mrs millers few out

14. Emilie was likely arranging her summer employment with a Mrs. Wister in Germantown. She may have been referring to Dr. Owen J. Wister and his wife, author Sarah Butler Wister. Dr. Wister had one of the busiest traveling practices, visiting patients throughout Germantown and northwest Philadelphia. Emilie left for Germantown on June 7, 1864, instead of June 1 as she had initially intended, and she continued working until September 20, 1864. Peitzman, "Lecture," 245–70.

15. The annual written examination of the graduating class of the ICY was administered, under the direction of Professor Pliney E. Chase, in May. Eleven students, including James M. Baxter Jr., Thomas H. Boling, J. Wesley Cromwell, Frank J. R. Jones, James H. Roberts, James L. Smallwood, Mary V. Brown, Harriet C. Johnson, Elizabeth Handy, Margaret A. Masten, and M. Gertrude Offitt, took the exam, answering questions in mathematics (geometry, plane trigonometry, and spherical trigonometry), Latin, and Greek. "Institute for Colored Youth," *Christian Recorder*, May 21, 1864.

WEDNESDAY, 4.

another bright day Mrs wister called to see Mrs Powel to day
I have Promised to go out on the 1st of June i will not get to The
exsominotion to at all nell went it was

THURSDAY, 5.

Very interesting Sue was here last night and vincent to day is quite
like summer I went down to Mr livelys but my mind was at the
samson st[16] hall i wanted to go to the aluni Sue and i

MAY, FRIDAY, 6, 1864.

went out soping yesterdy we went our bonnets in the evening we all
went to the School exersise at concert hall it was grand vincent come
home with us Nell was up a little while she is

SATURDAY, 7.

still thinking about egerton Nellie and Sue were both here this
morning in the evening i went down home found hidey Williams was
there i went for my bonnet it is beautiful

SUNDAY, 8.

it is a lovely morning how i would like to go to church morning
service is the last Part of the day i spent Part the evening in reading and
writing Bible class closed this evening at Mrs hawkinses very few out

MAY, MONDAY, 9, 1864.

very fine day but very warm i went down to mr livelys had a very
nice lesson then went down to school very few out i fear the girls are
losing their intrest in the school we had one name to report mr

TUESDAY, 10.

Seyers another warm day very busy Sue was here a little while in the
evening i went down home stoped at Nells she was not home i did
not go to see her meeting at aunt Nancys Nell wasnt there very

16. The paper described a season of
"soirees and concerts" held at the Sansom
Street Hall throughout the previous
winter. The author noted the particular
talents of the singers Aralena Purnell and
her younger sister Louisa. Emilie may
have wanted to attend a similar event at
the Sansom Street Hall. "Aralena Purnell,"
Christian Recorder, April 30, 1864.

WEDNESDAY, 11.

good meeting Pleasant to day Miss Williams and Mr and a Miss fry
called on me this morning Nellie did not come up as i expected this
evening a Miss Greenfeilds concert[17] comes off to night

MAY, THURSDAY, 12, 1864.

quite cloudy i went down to Mr livelys he was not home
consequently i lost another lesson I have not bin well all day i went
home and Put away some of my things in the evening i went down to
bustels [. . .]

FRIDAY, 13.

i spent the evening with Nell Sue was there we all went to the ice
cream saloon quite a dull day it comenced raining about evening
i have not bin out to day i received a very interesting letter frome

SATURDAY, 14.

Alfred yesterday i sent one to sister on Wednsday very showery
to day i was out in the after noon in the evening i went down home
found a letter there from mary williams

MAY, SUNDAY, 15, 1864.

quite an april day it has bin showering every little while I went to
church in the morning we had a very good sermon but i did not enJoy
it much as i had the toothach[18] the girls came up

17. On May 7 the *Recorder*
announced, "There will be a grand Concert
given on the 11th inst., at 7 ½ o'clock,
by Miss Greenfield, the celebrated 'Black
Swan,' assisted by the distinguished
Murio, of Philadelphia, and others."
Elizabeth Taylor Greenfield, known as
the "Black Swan," was born a slave in
Natchez, Mississippi. According to an 1855
biography, as a young child Greenfield was
moved from Mississippi to Philadelphia, where she was freed and raised by
Quakers. Greenfield was most well known
for her classical repertoire and was celebrated by abolitionists such as Frederick

Douglass and Harriet Beecher Stowe.
"Concert," *Christian Recorder*, May 7, 1864;
The Black Swan, 1–4; Lott, *Love and Theft*,
235.
18. Emilie's toothache persisted until
May 18, 1864. The nineteenth century
witnessed the founding of the first dental
college, first dental journal, and first dental society; the American Dental Convention was founded in Philadelphia in 1855.
It is unclear what caused Emilie's tooth
pain, but if it was the result of a cavity,
there were many materials used for fillings
that are far less common today. Dentists
were still experimenting with fillings such

FIGURE 15   Elizabeth Taylor Greenfield. Popularly known as the "Black Swan," Elizabeth Greenfield often performed at concerts and political gatherings. Photo from James Trotter, *Music and Some Highly Musical People* (Boston: Lee and Shepard, 1881), after page 66.

MONDAY, 16.

there was quite a growing riot[19] last night the boyes was in it John and vincent i have not bin well all day i went down to mr livelys but I did not go to school my tooth woud not

TUESDAY, 17.

let me i suffered very much last night with my face i have not bin able to to anything Nell came before waiting i was so sory i could not go

MAY, WEDNESDAY, 18, 1864.

my face is better to day lovely morning but rainy after noon Nell come up and spent a little while with me

THURSDAY, 19.

Pleasent i went down to Mr lively but did not take a lesson i went down there in the afternoon and staid their untill i went to the concert the concert[20] was spleen

FRIDAY, 20.

Did [splendid] the children all [. . .] sang well after the concert we all about [. . .] 8 in number went to the ice cream saloon through mr harrises kindness mr harris called from home we had to [. . .] go to the

MAY, SATURDAY, 21, 1864.

concert but i was afraid of taken cold butiful morning my two mentors have come the mormons i think three on me this morning Nell was up thi evening i did not go

as platinum, silver, asbestos, aluminum, amalgam—the most popular during the war—and tin. Glenner and Willey, "Dental Filling Materials," 71–75.

19. A riot broke out in Philadelphia at Seventh and Little Pine Streets. The men and women involved armed themselves with razors and threw bricks. What precipitated the riot is unknown. *Daily Age*, May 17, 1864.

20. A concert was held on May 17, 1864, at National Hall, with performances by the pupils of Lombard Street Public School, (colored) Fifth Section. The concert included various patriotic musical numbers, including solos, duets, quartets, and choruses. Tickets for the event were twenty-five cents each and the proceeds benefited the Sanitary Fair. "Concert," *Christian Recorder*, May 14, 1864.

SUNDAY, 22.

out lovely morning i did not go to church as i would liked to this
morning i went to church in the afternoon Dr Martin[21] Preached
he spoke Beutiful but most to lengthly in the evening Nel

MONDAY, 23.

and i went to central heard a very good sermon fine day Nell and Sue
were both here i went down to Mr livelys had quite a nice lesson then
went down to school and settled the business concerning the organ

MAY, TUESDAY, 24, 1864.

clear very busy all day Sue was a little while in the evening i went
home before meeting i heard such very Distressing news Poor Sonny
taylor died on Thursday lost in a fit Liz is quite from shock i went

WEDNESDAY, 25.

to meeting had a very good time not many out Thomas went up
home this morning Nellie was here this afternoon John was here
yesterday Mary and neal maggie BJ Ellen E and susy J Jay S were

THURSDAY, 26.

all here last evening and spent quite a Pleasent time very stormy
i have bin keep in by the rain all afternoon an evening I was sadly
disappointed i did not stop raining all the evening

MAY, FRIDAY, 27, 1864.

raining this morning again but cleard up in the afternoon I went down
home in the evening Sue and Nell came up here they had been out
shopping

SATURDAY, 28.

butiful day i have bin very busy in deed it very last [. . .] week up
at hayards for some time I went down have found a letter from
Brother A he is in Norfork va

21. Rev. John Sella Martin was a prominent minister noted in the *Recorder* for giving sermons from New York to Washington, D.C. On January 25, 1865, Martin lectured in Philadelphia, so he may have made an appearance at Emilie's church. "Washington Correspondence," *Christian Recorder*, July 9, 1864; "A Letter from New York," *Christian Recorder*, April 27, 1864.

FIGURE 16　The Reverend John Sella Martin. Rev. John Sella Martin was a former slave and minister of a church in Boston, Massachusetts. Courtesy of the Massachusetts Historical Society.

SUNDAY, 29.

it is a lovely morning i went to church we had a stranger to speake for us he spoke beutiful i really enjoyed his sermon in the afternoon Nell and I went to Johny Browns funeral[22]

MAY, MONDAY, 30, 1864.

lovely day I have bin quite busy to day getting ready to go away Mary went home to day i went up to the church in the evening i went down to mr livelys as usal then to school

TUESDAY 31.

quite Pleasant very busy all day in the evening we all went to st Thomases to [. . .] riely married then to Mr Tearband to meeting we had quite a well meeting

WEDNESDAY, 1.

to day has bin quite dull we had quit a large fire in our neoghborhood this afternoon school houses had their roofes burned off the fire was

JUNE, THURSDAY, 2, 1864.

below Els is quite wet i went down to mr livelys an recived my last lesson for the summer in the evening i regret to say i went with vincent to the odd

FRIDAY, 3.

fellows [. . .] i shall ever regret it they turned it in to a regular hall i have felt very uneasy all morning nell was very much opposed to my going she

SATURDAY, 4.

is very angry with me i went to the lecture last evening it seemed as if gibbs was talking to me in his discours vincent in all Nell and i went up to Bayards in the evening

---

22.   John E. Brown died on May 24, 1864, and was buried on May 29. Like Emilie's sister-in-law, Mary, Brown died of consumption, or tuberculosis. "Pennsylvania, Philadelphia City Death Certificates, 1803–1915," index and images, Family-Search, https://familysearch.org/pal:/MM9.1.1/J6PV-RLM (accessed May 16, 2013), John E. Brown, 1864.

JUNE, SUNDAY, 5, 1864.

this is a very solemn day it is communion we have had a very rainy day mr gibbs baby was Crisened this morning Eugene Jolly was down to church

MONDAY, 6.

beutiful morning i have bin busy geting ready to go to Germantown but it come up a shower since i did not go out i went down to school

TUESDAY, 7.

we had a very nice school this morning Philip and i started to germantown vincent was at the cars i not time hardly to speak to him i seemed safe it is very pleasent in Germantown

JUNE, WEDNESDAY, 8, 1864.

beutiful day i bin keep very busy since i have bin out here J sent a not to nellie to day it is quite lonsome out here I have Plenty time for thought and medataton

THURSDAY, 9.

rining this morning we have had rain for several thursdays but it cleard up in the afternoon i donnot have much idle time mrs wister is shure to find something for

FRIDAY, 10.

me as soon as i have finished one Peice she has another it is a lovely morning i received a letter from martin i do not quite like the tenor of it i also received mary Jones Potographes

JUNE, SATURDAY, 11, 1864.

it is like her but i did not receive it at first it has bine very Pleasent to day but it did not seem like Saturday i have only bin out once since i have bin here i miss going down home

SUNDAY, 12.

it is a lovely morning i did not go to church as i had to stay with the
boy[23] i spent Part of the morning in reading Crists sermon or the
mountain in the afternoon quite unecxpedly rachel [. . .] and

MONDAY, 13.

Pleiy came i was delighted we went out and quite a Pleasent walk
in the evening i went to church with miss grant heard a good sermon
i have Just answered Alfreds letter

JUNE, TUESDAY, 14, 1864.

very Pleasent not letter from home yet very [. . .] has bin some ever
sinc i have bin out here i how i would liked to go to meeting but i will
have to have meeting to

WEDNESDAY, 15.

myself very warm to day i have very few idle moments to day
i received a very Pleasent letter from Nell she telles me neal augustes
[. . .] married on Sunday morning

THURSDAY, 16.

and i belive mary is to be married to [. . .] night i received a letter
from mary williams to day i sent one to sarah I dont have time to be
lonesom out here

JUNE, FRIDAY, 17, 1864.

very warm to day i received a not from sarah saing Dave was Drafted
in the Country i answered nells note this evening

SATURDAY, 18.

I have bin very buisy all day and not very well i went out a little while
in the evening it is very unpleasent to go out the soldiers are [. . .]

---

23. Although "the boy" Emilie refers
to could not be identified, she may
have been referring to the Wisters' son,
Owen Jr. (called "Dan"), born in 1860.

Part of her responsibilities as a domestic
included taking care of the couple's child.
Peitzman, "Lecture," 245–70.

SUNDAY, 19.

beutiful morning i did not get through in time [. . .] to go to church
rachel came up and spent the morning with me in the afternoon
i went up to see Phery she has gone hom I went to church herd very
good exortotion after church i went to see miss ulman

JUNE, MONDAY, 20, 1864.

lovely morning rachel [. . .] brought my guitar out this morning
i hope i will find time to Practice this afternoon i spent over in wisters
with [. . .] in the evening we went

TUESDAY, 21.

down to mary wines lovly and had some strawberries i stole a few
minuts this morning to Practice here i have not Patience to tune it but
in the evening i went up miss winel

WEDNESDAY, 22.

very warm i am allmost out of Patience with my situation already it is
so confining here wednesday and nell is not com yet

JUNE, THURSDAY, 23, 1864.

very warm i [. . .] quite buisy as usal i do not think nell is coming out
this week I told mrs wister about her table [. . .] this morning

FRIDAY, 24.

i had a note from sarah this morning estelena was here this afternoon
i went down to the station with her i had quite a Pleasent walk

SATURDAY, 25.

this is i think the warmest day[24] we had have I went to town with
mrs wister to see the great Fair[25] i did not get home i was delightd
with the fair it was beutiful

24. A "warm spell" had hit Philadelphia, including "severe heat," with temperatures ranging from the mid-nineties
to one hundred degrees in some parts of
the city. An afternoon rain tempered the
extreme heat. "The Warm Spell," *Philadelphia Inquirer*, June 27, 1864, 3.

25. From June 7 to June 25, the
United States Sanitary Commission held
the Great Central Fair in Philadelphia,
which raised over $1.5 million to support
wounded soldiers and their families. The
Sanitary Commission held fairs across the
North in cities like Chicago, Cincinnati,

JUNE, SUNDAY, 26, 1864.

rather Pleasant to day i did not go to church during the day i spent the morning in reading and writing in the afternoon i went to see rachel in the evening we went to church

MONDAY, 27.

the evening it was very [. . .] I enjoyed myself very much yesterday i received a letter from nell at last saying she could not come out sue expect to go away this

TUESDAY, 28.

Week consequently i dont expect to see her very Pleasant to day how i whis [. . .] i could go to meeting this evening i amuse my Self by Practicing and reading if i had no my gatair

JUNE, WEDNESDAY, 29, 1864.

i think i would be very lonsome i am busy through the day and in the evening when it is not too warm i Practice this afternoon for the first i was out walking in t

THURSDAY, 30.

own [town] this is the last of June it has bin quite cloudy all day with a little rain in the afternoon it comenced Pouring this is my evening but I do not make much as of it

JULY, FRIDAY, 1.

this is the first very Pleasant this morning but we had a terriffick in the afternoon i play [. . .] in the evenings [. . .] the [. . .]

JULY, SATURDAY, 2, 1864.

quite cloudy all the morning i expect to go to twon this afternoon i started for town at 2 o it comenced raining Just as i got out of the car

---

and Boston to raise funds to support the care of wounded soldiers and to encourage patriotic devotion. "Great Central Fair," *Christian Recorder*, April 30, 1864. Gallman, "Voluntarism in Wartime," 93–116.

Emilie also elaborated on her visit to the fair in the memoranda section of her diary for 1864, where she comments on the absence of handiwork on display produced by women of color.

SUNDAY, 3.

lovely day i went to church in the morning heard a good sermon
we stoped at aunt Janes and to see rachel she is quite sick vincent ever
kind came up for [. . .] stoped in to bustles egr

MONDAY, 4.

ton [egerton] was there looking like a lost sheep i started for
germantown about half Past 5 in the afternoon i went out with dave
i felt very lonsome in the evening

JULY, TUESDAY, 5, 1864.

fine day but very warm Mrs. Wister went to town with dave she
could not dou a better thing i have bin quite busy all day how i would
like to go

WEDNESDAY, 6.

to a meeting very much quite Pleasent this morning but in the
afternoon very warm I did not have much time to Practice to day very
busy i sent a note to Sarah

THURSDAY, 7.

on tuesday exceedingly warm today in the afternoon it comenced
raining Martin was at town on Sunday he stoped at the house but i
did not see him

JULY, FRIDAY, 8, 1864.

very warm this morning i had a talk with mrs about the all absorbing
topic i went to nell and liz today I see i will not be able to spend the
sumer in germantown

SATURDAY, 9.

rather cloudy and warm we were all called up this morning to receive
our ration of supper i talk mrs wister this i would have little use for it
i went down to

SUNDAY, 10.

Marys to tell her neil It is a beautiful morning i could not go to church
home all the afternoon I spent the afternoon in reading in the evening
i went to church they had no Preaching

JULY, MONDAY, 11, 1864.

after church i went home with becky smith mr Johnson was with
me exceedingly warm to day i was out this afternoon stoped to see
Miss uhman Rachel come and spent the evening

TUESDAY, 12.

with me very warm I have had my first lesson on the sewing
machine[26] suceeded admireablely I worked all the afternoon no word
from home this week as yet

WEDNESDAY, 13.

very pleasant to day i had been Practicing a little on the machine
no word from nell yet in the evening mary m and i went to see rachel
and spent quite a Pleas [Pleasant]

JULY, THURSDAY, 14, 1864.

time quite pleasent I tought i certainly would get a letter to day but
no letter as yet I am porly looking for vincent this evening but he did
not come

FRIDAY, 15.

cool this morning but pleasent quite busy all day I Practse a little
to day Rachel was here this afternoon this evening likely smith and
anna came up and spent quite a nice

SATURDAY, 16.

little time I had a letter from him this week I have been sick to day
last night i wrote a lett to lenox I was out a few squares this afternoon
i received a letter from sister and

26. Accomplished seamstresses like Emilie acquainted themselves with the sewing machine, patented in 1846, with some reservation, as machines were expensive and often owned by subcontractors who paid women low wages. Social investigator Virginia Penny published a report in 1863 in which she described the physical strain on women who sewed on machines for long hours. "It produces a pain first in the hips, and the jar affects the nerves; and the sameness of the stitch on white or black goods produces a constant strain of the eye." Stansell, *City of Women*, 113–15. Penny, *Employments of Women*, 311.

JULY, SUNDAY, 17, 1864.

a Potograph from my Dear Brother in [. . .] beutiful morning home
as usal but i shall in devor [endeavor] to improve my time by reading
i have bin quite sick to day i am sorry to say i have not time to
Church to day

MONDAY, 18.

Pleasent this morning I feel very much as if i would like to be home
aunt mary went home to day i received a letter from Nell to day at
long last i am not very [. . .]

TUESDAY, 19.

Pleased with it quit warm i have bin running the machine nearly all
day to day in the afternoon dave and i went to take a walk i was very
glad after siting all day

JULY, WEDNESDAY, 20, 1864.

exceedingly warm to day busy as usal i have bin worried conciderable
to day with the machine in the evening Mary M and i went to see
becky and anna we had

THURSDAY, 21.

a lovely time quite Pleasent to day i wrote to liz to day I had Plenty of
visiters this afternoon rachel miss uhman and miss wood i feel very
low spirited to night[27]

FRIDAY, 22.

owing to disapointement very much like rain to day wich is very
much needed i went down to Maryes this evening my only place of
risort rachel lives so far that I can not go to see

27. During the summer of 1864, Emilie described herself as "low spirited" and mentioned other depressive emotions. Based on her extensive research on African American women's labor, historian Jacqueline Jones found that "in the countryside, black women domestics suffered from desperate isolation in the absence of a larger community." The seclusion Emilie experienced in her summer job placements might account for her low spirits. Jones, *American Work*, 284.

JULY, SATURDAY, 23, 1864.

her often i wrote to nell yesterday i may expect an answer about next week not of my many friends have bin out to see me yeat i have bin sick all day

SUNDAY, 24.

very Pleasent I went to church this morning the first Sunday i have realy enjoyed since i have bin out here i hear a beutiful sermon after church i went to see rachel i wrote to sis

MONDAY, 25.

ter [sister] yesterday Mary came up and spent the evening last evening i recieved a letter from Nelly to day it was rather Different from the last one i had a nice time Practicing

JULY, TUESDAY, 26, 1864.

in the evening quite Pleasent to day i have bin a busy as usal i answered Nells letter this evening rachel was up i went to Maryes and spent a Pleasent time

WEDNESDAY, 27.

it thos we gon to get warm again lizzie eloisan in town i would like to see her I was out early this evening went over to miss uhmans then to sawmakers lane

THURSDAY, 28.

exceedingly warm this morning sarah Jones was out here but not to see me vincent came out this evening i was Pleased to see him we went over to

JULY, FRIDAY, 29, 1864.

see miss uhman liz has gone to see uncle william very warm to day quite like august anna and her friend were to see me this evening

SATURDAY, 30.

very warm i have bin busy as usal doing little of everything and not much of anything mary was this evening

SUNDAY, 31.

lovely morning i did not go to church very warm in the evening
i went down to rachels we went to the luthrian [Lutheran] Church
after church we stoped in marys

AUGUST, MONDAY, 1, 1864.

quite sultry i have had no letter from home since i came out this last
time mary was up this evening if was not for her it would be quite
dull

TUESDAY, 2.

very warm with rain wich is much needed i recieved a letter to day
from sue quite unexpectedly i spent the evening with

WEDNESDAY, 3.

mary Pleasent to day in the afternoon i went up to see estelena but
she had gon i went down to maryes it comenced raining i spent

AUGUST, THURSDAY, 4, 1864.

the evening with her she gave me a excellent tea wich is very rare out
here i answerd maryes letter this evening i have had no time to Putter
to day

FRIDAY, 5.

very warm to day the excitement still continues about the rebels[28] the
girls here over from shoemakers lane we went down to maryes

SATURDAY, 6.

not quite as warm as yesterday more did i went home in the [. . .]
rain found then all well Nell was glad to see me i went to bustils

28.   Emilie may have been referring to the Confederate invasion at Hagerstown, Maryland, and the threat of invasion at the Pennsylvania border. On August 6, 1864, the *Inquirer* reported that Governor Andrew Curtin had received dispatches from Hagerstown that Confederate troops were again advancing toward Pennsylvania. In the days prior to August 5, speculation about the potential for invasion had littered newspaper headlines. However, on August 8, 1864, the Confederates retreated back to Shepherdstown, part of the newly formed state of West Virginia. "The New Invasion. 5000 Rebels at Hagerstown," *Philadelphia Inquirer*, August 6, 1864; "Our Harrisburg Letter," *Philadelphia Inquirer*, August 9, 1864; see also various articles in the August 5, 1864, edition of the *Philadelphia Inquirer*.

AUGUST, SUNDAY, 7, 1864.

I feel so happy to be permitted to worship in my own church
mr [. . .] spoke in the morning mr gibbs Delivered a Powerful Sermon
in the afternoon i

MONDAY, 8.

spent this Sundy very Pleasent day i out this morning in the [. . .]
henry and vincent [. . .] the [. . .] Martin came out here this
afternoon

TUESDAY, 9.

he met a Cold reseption i had a letter from Tomy and answer it
i expected Nell and barker out last night

AUGUST, WEDNESDAY, 10, 1864.

very [. . .] all day i have not bin very busy i thout i could not stand
the heat I did go out untill evening i went over to [. . .] i had a
Peleasent time i went to maryes we went

THURSDAY, 11.

down the lane very warm i did not go out this evening in the
afternoon i went to take a little walk i spent Part of the evening in
Practiceing i sent a note to Nells [. . .]

FRIDAY, 12.

not inite as [. . .] to day as has bin busy as usol in the evening the
girls came up may and I went to walk with them they are very wild

AUGUST, SATURDAY, AUGUST 13, 1864.

very sultry to day the is almost in toloreable but we must bear it
i have not heard anything from home i have not seen rachel we have
a very heavy showing

SUNDAY, 14.

this evening lovely morning after the rain i did not go to church in
the morning vincent & Dave came out this morning Paid me quite a
Pleasent visit in the evening i went to church

MONDAY, 15.

with mrs leninns things goine as usal mary was up she is my only
companion out here

AUGUST, TUESDAY, 16, 1864.

quite pleasant to day to day i have bin sewing on the machine it give
me a great deal of trouble I have bin very buisy sewing this evening
i finished my dress

WEDNESDAY, 17.

body at last quite warm agan [. . .] i had a letter from nell yesterday
we quite a heavy shower this afternoon in the evening we went
to see

THURSDAY, 18.

Rachel but she had not got home yet i left a letter for her the girls
were over this evening mary was here

AUGUST, FRIDAY, 19, 1864.

I received a huge letter to day from Alfred it is almost like a news
paper he gives me a full descriptin [description] of what he is doing
while he is away

SATURDAY, 20.

It has bin exceedingly cool to day almost like fall i have bin so try
this day with my charge that i am ready to run away before my time
is out

SUNDAY, 21.

very Pleasent this morning I have bin quite sick all day i have not bin
well enough to go to church rachel was here in the morning out [. . .]
did mary in the

AUGUST, MONDAY, 22, 1864.

evening Pleasent i received a letter from town to day EJ has not
written To me how Dave [. . .] i attended to write to neell but did
not finish

TUESDAY, 23.

Rachel was here this morning brought me a letter from [. . .] i do not feel like answering it at Present i succeded in finishing nells later this morning miss uhman

WEDNESDAY, 24.

brought me a letter that i ough[t] of had weekes ago quite Pleasent i went Down in the cars this afternoon to see rachel ni the evening mary and went to a

AUGUST, THURSDAY, 25, 1864.

Festival i had a great deal of fun the country gents were very gd Cant the ladies [. . .] most of them were Dressed as if for a Party I expected vincent This evening but he

FRIDAY, 26.

did not come out Pleasant to day everything goes on Pretty much as usol I feel Discontent with my self I know i do not read my bible or meditate as much as i ought but i am

SATURDAY, 27.

resolved to try to do better I have not heard from Nell i expect she thinks she will not write because i am Coming in soon mean thing

AUGUST, SUNDAY, 28, 1864.

very Pleasant this morning i did not go to Church i expected rachel but she did not Com up I am reading a book caled immovably decided reason very interesting i wrote a long letter

MONDAY, 29.

to alfred this morning Comenced one to will quite Pleasant to day i received a letter from EJ he herd from [. . .] i went to Church last evening up to

TUESDAY, 30.

the [. . .] i made mary go up with me i have learned two little Peices in our Sineing book did the [. . .]

AUGUST, WEDNESDAY, 31, 1864.

lovely day rachel and i [. . .] to go out together but she Could not go
i vincent to take a [. . .] spent the evening very [. . .] maryes i [. . .]

THURSDAY, 1.

he [. . .] some in deed with out her this is the first of fall very
Pleasaent vincent came out to see me quite unexpected I expeced EJ
but he did not get here

FRIDAY, 2.

quite cool this morning i had a very sad letter from sister to day
it made me feel very badly Father is quite feable[29] I finished writing to
Wil this evening

SEPTEMBER, SATURDAY, 3, 1864.

cloudy to day i went to the city this afternoon i stoped at the shoes
makers and rachels it comenced rain

SUNDAY, 4.

ing [raining] very rainy morning i was quite disapponted i did not
go to church in the morning it rained in the afternoon but i went to
church we

MONDAY, 5.

only had two tables very good exortation i spent the evening very
Pleasent [. . .] came out in the train [. . .] it all day away all the
evening i received

SEPTEMBER, TUESDAY, 6, 1864.

a letter from EJ saing he would be out raining still mary did not come
up this evening i expect Nell forster and vincent out on

WEDNESDAY, 7.

Thursday quite pleasent i went up to the Depot met Estelena then
went to see Caroline She is sinking very fast i think i spent the
evening

29. Emilie's father was sixty-four
years old. His illness brought additional

concern, perhaps, about his mortality and
the distance she had to travel to see him.

THURSDAY, 8.

with Mary rachel goes away on Saturday rather cloudy Nellie came out but Mr foster did not vincent came we spent quite a Pleasent evening

SEPTEMBER, FRIDAY, 9, 1864.

quite like fall to day i feel very lone spirited and worried i went up town this evening i have very little recreation out here

SATURDAY, 10.

quite warm again i have a letter from tomy on thursdy this afternoon don and i taken very long walk

SUNDAY, 11.

rainy day but not quite as hard as last Sunday i went to church in the morning herd a good sermon

SEPTEMBER, MONDAY, 12, 1864.

Clear morning school comences this evening how i would like to be in town[30] i was down to maryes this afternoon Dav

TUESDAY, 13.

on [Davon] i were out for a walk i wrote to Sister on Sunday and to tomy i very ansious about father i have not

WEDNESDAY, 14.

had an answer from either of my letters i very [. . .] Disapponted to day nell sent me a note saying mary was coming out with foster I expected to go

SEPTEMBER, THURSDAY, 15, 1864

go in the evening to a Party got all ready and was disaponted lovely day to day vincent came in the evening he was not

---

30. According to an 1864 report by the ICY, 114 students attended the school, including 25 boys and 41 girls in the high school and 16 boys and 32 girls in the preparatory school. Classes at the high school level included Greek, Latin, mathematics, chemistry, and natural philosophy. "Annual Report of the Managers of the Institute for Colored Youth," *Christian Recorder*, October 8, 1864.

FRIDAY, 16.

well foster paid me quite a Pleasent visit on wednesdy evening I have bin quite industrious to day and evening mary b did not com

SATURDAY, 17.

up very Pleasent morning i have felt very happy all morning i hope i am not going to hear any bad news

SEPTEMBER, SUNDAY, 18, 1864.

very Pleasent i was home all day in the evening i went to see caroline then went to church i heard a very good sermon

MONDAY, 19.

lovely morning i am waiting Paitenty for my freedom from germontown in the evening mary and i went to livelys spent quite a Pleasen

TUESDAY, 20.

t [Pleaseant] time I feel gay and happy i expect to go home to day no girl came up but i taken french [. . .] I went to meeting

SEPTEMBER, WEDNESDAY, 21, 1864.

enjoyed the meeting very much I have bin very busy putting away my Clothes in the afternoon i went to help make mourning for the Poor

THURSDAY, 22.

little orphan in the evening mr foster taken nell and i to the festival[31] mr Steward[32] was buried to day he was taken to the church Mr gibbs Spoke very well over him

31. On Wednesday, September 21, 1864, the Central Presbyterian Church on Lombard Street, approximately a half mile from Emilie's Seventh Street Presbyterian Church, held "a grand concert," according to the *Recorder*. The students of the Sabbath School, under the direction of "renowned Professor A. Burris," performed in the packed church. After the concert, ladies from the church provided refreshments in the church basement. While Emilie mentioned attending a festival in her entry for Thursday, September 22, she may have been referring to the Wednesday concert. "Presbyterian Church, Lombard Street," *Christian Recorder*, September 24, 1864.

32. Samuel Steward's death certificate indicates that he died of hemorrhaging lungs. "Pennsylvania, Philadelphia City Death Certificates, 1803–1915," index and images, FamilySearch, https://familysearch.org/pal:/MM9.1.1/JXY5-9PG (accessed May 8, 2013), Samuel Steward, 1864.

FRIDAY, 23.

very busy all day getting ready to go see Father in the evening i went to meeting very few out some missionary from africa spoke foster was there he is quite a beau

SEPTEMBER, SATURDAY, 24, 1864.

busy as usal i will not get off to day quite excitement this afternoon mr green was molested[33] and defended himself by shooting one of his assailants he was arreseted nell and I had a talk with Sue

SUNDAY, 25.

quite cool this morning but Pleasent i went to church heard very good sermon stoped at aunt Janes vincent was with us church in the afternoon in the evening we were Disappointed vincent did

MONDAY, 26.

not come and foster went to church vincent come late busy washing to I went out in the afternoon stoped at mr livelys and mrs [. . .] vincent was down to tell me Caroline was dead[34] he

SEPTEMBER, TUESDAY, 27, 1864.

was down in the evening brought me some cream he was very affectionate lovely day I started for harrisburg at half Past 2 had a very tiresom Journey I [. . .] about so found all well Father

33. The *Recorder* reported that when Alfred Green, sergeant major in the 127th USCT, was assaulted by ruffians, he fended off the men first by pistol-whipping them. When the men did not desist, Green shot one of them in the leg. The paper was even more indignant that Green was arrested alongside his assailants, but the officer was released the next day. "The majority of the people with whom we have conversed upon the subject," the paper reported, "regret that the ball [i.e., the bullet] did not hit a vital part." Alfred M. Green served with the 127th until his discharge in February 1865. "Assault on Sergeant-Major Green," *Christian Recorder*, October 1, 1864. Bates, *History of Pennsylvania Volunteers*, 1125.

34. According to her death certificate, Caroline Miller died of tuberculosis on September 26, 1864. "Pennsylvania, Philadelphia City Death Certificates, 1803–1915," index and images, FamilySearch, https://familysearch.org/pal:/MM9.1 .1/JXYB-DWY (accessed May 8, 2013), Caroline Miller, 1864.

WEDNESDAY, 28.

was delighted to see me rainy day i am in for the day i expect
father has gone to the Depot I went around to mary williams and to
Chesters this evening it is very

THURSDAY, 29.

well up here raining again this morning but clear in the afternoon was
out a little while alex was to come around but he did not come

SEPTEMBER, FRIDAY, 30, 1864.

it rained very hard last night very cloudy this morning I sent a letter
home yesterday i went down to see mr burke and stoped at Chesters
took tea

OCTOBER, SATURDAY, 1.

after tea we went to spences then to the celler to is the first of oct
very raw and cold i have bin home all day not one of the girls have
bin to see me but I enjo

SUNDAY, 2.

y [enjoy] fathers society very much i read to him and talk to him
makes the time Pass another dull day i did not get to church untill
evening father went

OCTOBER, MONDAY, 3, 1864.

to church i was so Pleased to see him there this morning i spent [. . .]
with mary and Mr Fry the afternoon be went out [. . .] was with us
in the

TUESDAY, 4.

evening i went ou to margies cloudy but not raining I went to see neal
off Poor nell i sympathize with her spent the day and evening out

WEDNESDAY, 5.

still cloudy i received a letter from Nell yesterday Saying she was
going away on Thursday she wants me to come home but i shant go
untill

OCTOBER, THURSDAY 6, 1864.

Saturday if noth happins home all the morning in the afternoon
i went up to Mrs sanders i spent quite a Plesent time i had tow [two]
gentelmen to

FRIDAY, 7.

gallant me home little Alex was my main gallant clear the first
morning we have since i have bin here had Chester and i were out
walking after i

SATURDAY, 8.

went to spencers spent quite a Plesent time lovely day i stoped at
Mrs burkes and Chesters i started for home about 20 [. . .] at 6 in the
evening we all went to see the torch light Procesion[35]

OCTOBER, SUNDAY 9, 1864.

quite Pleasant but very windy i did not go to church in the morning
in the afternoon Mr gibbs Preached a very good sermon I spent the
evening at home vincent came

MONDAY, 10.

up fine day i have bin Promanading to day i was to see Bayards
I expect to go there on tuesday i went down to school very few out
not more than a half

TUESDAY, 11.

dozen quite Pleasant I received a letter from Ellen this morning
i answered it i wrote to sister i have comenced my winter ocupation
i did not go to

---

35. The National Union Party, the party of Abraham Lincoln and Andrew Johnson in the presidential election of 1864, held a large torchlight rally in Independence Square on the evening of October 8, 1864. The *Public Ledger* noted that in addition to former Pennsylvania governor William Johnston and Philadelphia mayor Alexander Henry, the rally was attended by "ladies in large numbers." Mayor Henry stated that the issue before the nation was "between manhood and dishonor," referring in particular to the burning of Chambersburg at the hands of Confederate general Jubal Early in late July. "Union Meeting and Torchlight Procession," *Public Ledger*, October 10, 1864.

OCTOBER, WEDNESDAY 12, 1864.

meeting I feel so very lonsome with out Nell if she stayes all winter i dont know what i shall do raining all day clear in the eve

THURSDAY, 13.

ning [evening] very Pleasent i went down to mr livelys this morning i did not get out untill quite late in the evening lizzie and i went

FRIDAY, 14.

to a Political meeting it was very interesting home as usal on Fridays no word of Nells coming

OCTOBER, SATURDAY 15, 1864.

i stoped home this evening found [. . .] Craige there it seemed very strang not to stop in Blacks

SUNDAY, 16.

very fine day i went to Church in the morning heard an excelent sermon stoped several Places then went home for the rest of the day liz taken tea with

MONDAY, 17.

me vincent spent the evening he is as indefenite as ever i went to mr livelys I was quite disapponted in my lesson we had quite an enteresting school

OCTOBER, TUESDAY, 18, 1864.

Pleasent to day another meeting on hand to night i was disapponted i did not get to Prayer meeting but i had an opportunity to Practice

WEDNESDAY, 19.

a little self denia i need it very much I have bin [. . .] crossed a great deal to day i feel all most sick i expected the girls up this even

THURSDAY, 20.

ing [evening] but they did not come i went to mr livelys this morning home most of the afternoon in the evening i went to the concert had to march

OCTOBER, FRIDAY, 21, 1864.

i had a letter from Nell on Thursday Nann and Miss [. . .] were in
here a

SATURDAY, 22.

quite stormy all day i stoped home in the evening Mon did not get off
liz williams came with i was there she is looking very well

SUNDAY, 23.

rather cloudy this morning i did not go to Church this morning mon
and i went in the afternoon and in the evening we went to central[36]
vincent went with us

OCTOBER, MONDAY, 24, 1864.

fine day i have bin buisy as usal in the evening i went to Mr livelys then
to school oh how [. . .] I miss Nell i feel lost and unhappy without her

TUESDAY, 25.

clear i must realy write to nell this evening she will think all kinds of
things meeting at our house Pretty good meeting vincent came just as
it was out after mee

WEDNESDAY, 26.

ting [meeting] i wrote a long letter to nellie how i wish i could feel
satisfied about some certain things i am living in an uncertian state
from time to time

OCTOBER, THURSDAY, 27, 1864

i do not care to go out i feel so lost i went to mr livelys this morning
I am always glad when my lesson is done our thursdayes I stopped at
hecs and aunt Janes

FRIDAY, 28.

and at bustils spent a Dull evening at home vincent came about 10
i came up here i have bin exceedingly busy this evening fixing up our
Part of the house i expected

36. "Central" likely refers to the Central Presbyterian Church.

SATURDAY, 29.

kate ligtle up here but she did not come i did not get home as I usaly
do i was to buisy and the streets were to rowdy the Democrats[37] had
the rowdy Prossion

OCTOBER, SUNDAY, 30, 1864.

lovely morning i went to church herd a very good sermon I have an
unhappy feeling i cant account for it after church vincent and I stoped
it aunt Janes vincent came up in the evening

MONDAY, 31.

quite cold to day nothing of intress occurd to day in the evening
I went to mr livelys then to school ive had a nice school several
strangers down

NOVEMBER, TUESDAY, 1.

to day is a holliaday[38] with most ever y one the Colored soldiers are
in and everything seemes cherful i went to meeting quite a nice little
meeting after meeting we went

NOVEMBER, WEDNESDAY, 2, 1864.

to see the [. . .] at head quarters I have had no letter from nell this
week she is [. . .] in a hury to answer my letters

THURSDAY, 3.

Cloudy i went as usual to mr livelys i cant say i improve much he
thinks i do stoped in bustills [. . .] spending the evening meal was at
our house vincent

37. Democrats held torchlight rallies
in advance of the presidential election
of 1864 in support of their candidates,
former general in chief of the Army of the
Potomac George McClellan—a Philadelphian by birth—and Ohio congressman
George Pendleton. An advertisement
in the October 22, 1864, edition of the
Daily Age called on Democrats to attend
a procession that evening and to bring
"banners and torches!" The "rowdy"
Democratic rally Emilie described on
October 29 turned violent, resulting in the

death of James Campbell. A reward offer
for information leading to Campbell's
murderer ran in the November 19, 1864,
edition of the Daily Age. "Victory!," Daily
Age, October 22, 1864; "Reward Offered,"
Daily Age, November 19, 1864.

38. On November 1, 1864, Maryland
adopted a new state constitution that
outlawed slavery. Emilie elaborates on
these events on December 7, 1864, and in
her memoranda pages, where she refers to
the emancipation of Maryland.

FRIDAY, 4.

came for me he comes as regular as can be i dont see what he means
i have not courage to se him i received a letter from tomy yesterday
he did not say anything about

NOVEMBER, SATURDAY, 5, 1864.

coming home here is the last of the weeke and no letter from Ellen
i think she has set me down as one of the small things in her opinion
if i do not hear from her soon

SUNDAY, 6.

i shall act according beutiful day i was not out in the morning but i
tried to spend my time Profitible in the afternoon i went to church
sunrise Preached for us in the evening

MONDAY, 7.

i stoped at home vincent came up very [. . .] i went too mr livelys
then to the meeting we had no school we had quite a nice time at the
meeting vincent was there

NOVEMBER, TUESDAY, 8, 1864.

rainy angain to day to day is the great election i think lincoln[39] will
gain the day i did not go to meeting for fer [fear] somthing might
happeen

WEDNESDAY, 9.

Ellan came home yesterday morning did not come up to see untill this
evening i fear i will have to hold that against her i was delighted to
see her never the less she spent the

THURSDAY, 10.

evening with me it has bin a very stormy week i will [strikethrough]
not get out to day i went down to mr livelys he did not give me a
new lesson Nell was up vincent came up he

---

39. On November 8, 1864, Abraham
Lincoln was reelected president, a vote
that ensured that the war would continue.
Lincoln's victory was by no means assured

in the months prior to the election,
as George McClellan was running on the
Democratic ticket in favor of ending the
war as quickly as possible.

NOVEMBER, FRIDAY, 11, 1864.

did not expect to see Nellie up here want to see how he will act now
Nell has come home Poor egerton i know he feels good Nell and i had
a real tromp to day

SATURDAY, 12.

i went to the lecture in the evening it was very interesting very busy
all i did not get home this evening

SUNDAY, 13.

Bitter cold day i went to church in the morning heard a very good
sermon stop at Mr gibbs after church spent the after noon at home
Nell come up vincent did not come

NOVEMBER, MONDAY, 14, 1864.

up untill late quite wintery i went to mr livelys then to school had
Pretty good school Peterson came Part of the way home with me
vincent did not he left to [. . .]

TUESDAY, 15.

very wet and Disagreeable i went to meeting very few out i am sorry
to have to say vincent ever Constant

WEDNESDAY, 16.

Dull and rainy i have not bin out i have bin quite industryes this
evening i have sewed a great deal and and Practiced quite much Nell
was up

NOVEMBER, THURSDAY, 17, 1864.

very damp and Disagreable to [. . .] we were to go up town but the
weather Prevented I spent quit an agreeable evening at home sewing
came get vincent thre as

FRIDAY, 18.

usual rainy all day very fast i leaft vincent last night it was quite late
almost 12 [. . .] go

SATURDAY, 19.

Dull this morning clear in the afternoon i stoped home a letter was a waiting from tomy

NOVEMBER, SUNDAY, 20, 1864.

quite dull i went to church in the after noon it rand quite hard towards evening i spent the evening with nell

MONDAY, 21.

rainy all day EJ came in here quite sick this after noon frightend me much he had not gone longe when [strikethrough] Alfred[40] come looking like a salor indeed

TUESDAY, 22.

i went down to mr livelys it raind[41] very hard indeed then to school i got very wet cought a bad cold meeting at mrs redds i did not go I was not

NOVEMBER, WEDNESDAY, 23, 1864.

well quite sick all day but had to iron wich did not improve my health barker came up and spent quite a Pleasent evening with me Nell did not

THURSDAY, 24.

come quite cold to day olways cold on thanksgiving day I went to churhc in the afternoon was Disapponted mr gibbs was not out he was sick quite a number out in the

40. This appears to be Alfred's first furlough after a year in service. His return home must have been bittersweet, coming as it did on the first anniversary of his wife's death. Alfred served on the USS *Mount Vernon*, which participated in the Union blockade off North Carolina. In May 1864, the *Mount Vernon* fought the *Raleigh*, a Confederate ironclad near Wilmington. Department of the Navy, Naval History and Heritage Command, http://www.history.navy.mil/photos/sh-usn/usnsh-m/mt-vern.htm.

41. The *Inquirer* reported that heavy rain had caused the Schuylkill River to rise and parts of the city were flooded. The *Recorder* reminded readers that dressing for the weather and keeping legs and feet dry and warm were essential for fighting illness. "Effect of the Heavy Rain," *Philadelphia Inquirer*, November 23, 1864. Dr. Dio Lewis, "Talks about Health," *Christian Recorder*, November 26, 1864.

FRIDAY, 25.

evening we went to mr livelys concert vincent taken me and barker nell after the concert we went to lyons went mrs [. . .] on there me Played the agreable

NOVEMBER, SATURDAY, 26, 1864.

rainy day again Alfred was up this afternoon in the evening i was quite supprised to see vincent he came up and spent the evening

SUNDAY, 27.

lovely morning i went to church a stranger from the institute spoke for us i was not very well i did not get oppertunity to hear much Nell come up ear

MONDAY, 28.

ly [early] we had quite an old time Chat about matters and things clear i went to mr livelys knew my lesson went to school then to bethel to a meeting[42] very interes

NOVEMBER, TUESDAY, 29, 1864.

ting [interesting] meeting at mrs whites quite a number out but i am sorry to say the meeting seemed quite cold and spiritless Nellie did not go vincent was absent

WEDNESDAY, 30.

quite warm busy as usal Alfred came up and stayed a little while i sent a letter to tom on Sunday Nellie did not com up this evening

DECEMBER, THURSDAY, 1.

the first day of the winter so called very Pleasant Nell and i went out shoping i succeeded in Purchasing my Dress spent Part of the evening home grand

---

42. John M. Langston, "a gentleman of much literary distinction" and the president of the National Union Rights League, spoke at Mother Bethel African Methodist Episcopal Church at Sixth and Lombard Streets with "no ordinary merit and ability." "Personal," *Christian Recorder*, December 3, 1864.

FRIDAY, 2.

went down to aunt Janes Alfred come up for me to go to the [. . .]
but i Could not go very Disagreeable out

SATURDAY, 3.

very damp but not raining i went home and stoped at Nells barker
was there

SUNDAY, 4.

cold I did not go out in the morning communion in the afternoon very
happy meeting was here several tables after curch we stoped at aunt
Janes in the evening and went to

DECEMBER, MONDAY, 5, 1864.

st Thomas heard the revrin mr Cooper quite cold i went to mr livelys
then to school we had a very good school after school we apponted a
committe to solicit donations

TUESDAY, 6.

Cold i was down home a few minutes this morning meeting at
mrs smiths more out than usaly Come out vincent was about as usal
we went around to Shiloh park after meeting

WEDNESDAY, 7.

very Stormy vincent gave me coupel of tickets and for Nell we went
to the Celabration[43] it certainly was a very grand afair the singing and
speaking was exellent

DECEMBER, THURSDAY, 8, 1864.

quite Cold and windy I went down to mr livelys but he was so
fatigued he Could not give me a lesson i went to mrs offerts to [. . .]
and [. . .] i cam

---

43. The *Recorder* noted that on
Wednesday, December 7, a "large portion
of our colored citizens assembled in
National Hall," located on Market Street,
to celebrate emancipation in Maryland.
Rev. J. C. Gibbs's speech was met with
loud applause. Emilie notes the end of
slavery in Maryland in her entry for
November 1, 1864, and elaborates on it
in her memoranda pages. "Celebration of
the Emancipation in Maryland," *Christian
Recorder*, December 17, 1864.

FRIDAY, 9.

home about eight i only was out in the afternoon yesterday vincent spent the evening with me he comes very to reagular but there is no understanding between us Alfred was up this afternoon

SATURDAY, 10.

we had quite a snow storm last night but it soon will be gone when the sun makes his appearance Nell was up here this evening it was so disagreeble i did not go Down

DECEMBER, SUNDAY, 11, 1864.

very stormy i did not go to Church in the morning not out all unsusal thing for me Ellen did not Come up vincent came spent the evening

MONDAY, 12.

very Colld but Clear i went to mr livelys he was not home he did not Com to school we had quite a sociable school

TUESDAY, 13.

Cloudy Ellen Came up and spent the day liz stoped before meeting we all went togeather had a very good meeting quite a number out

DECEMBER, WEDNESDAY, 14, 1864.

home all day no one Came up very busy with my Dress Nell did not Come up

THURSDAY, 15.

I was at mr livelys as usal this morning quite Cold in the afternoon Nell and vincent shoping stoped at bustils spent the evening home

FRIDAY, 16.

[Blank]

DECEMBER, SATURDAY, 17, 1864.

[Blank]

SUNDAY, 18.

quite Cold i was at Church in the afternoon it Comenced raining right after church I did not go to Church in the evening my throat being sore

MONDAY, 19.

quite a rainy day my throat very sore i did not get to mr lively or to school quite a Disappontment vincent stoped after school gave me a ticket

DECEMBER, TUESDAY, 20, 1864.

quite Pleasent was at meeting at aunt Nancys excellent Meeting everyone seemed in the right spirit after meeting i went to the fair[44] very nice

WEDNESDAY, 21.

very Disagreeable to day quite a snow storm i have not bin out i saw school friends from harrisburg promentamery there i was miss spence [. . .] of Harrisburg

THURSDAY, 22.

bitter Cold day i was not very well but i went down to mr livelys in the moring in the afternoon i went to bustiles and several other Places barker was along we

DECEMBER, FRIDAY, 23, 1864.

had a great deal of fun in the evening we went to the fair I have bin busy all Day trying to finish my Dress vincent was up i Did not

SATURDAY, 24.

expect him after treating him so badly very busy all day i went out about 8 went down home then to the fair i had an eggnough Drinking in the evening we had quite a nice time

---

44. Over the holidays in December 1864, Philadelphia's black community celebrated with "a perfect and almost endless round of Fairs, Festivals, Suppers and social evening parties within the limits of our own fair city of Brotherly Love," according to the *Recorder*. Fairs were held by several churches Emilie visited or mentioned, including Bethel Church on Sixth and Lombard Streets and St. Thomas (African) Protestant Episcopal Church at Fifth and Adelphi Streets, and other fairs and festivals were held at churches near Emilie's home, like the A.M.E. Wesley Church on Hurst Street between Lombard and South Streets and between Fifth and Sixth Streets and the Wesley Methodist Church on Lombard Street, between Sixth and Fifth Streets. "City Notices," *Christian Recorder*, January 7, 1865; Catto, *A Semi-Centenary Discourse*, 106–7.

SUNDAY, 25.

Christmas[45] has come at last home in the morning in the afternoon i went to Church herd a very good sermon in the evening i had several [. . .] we spent quite

DECEMBER, MONDAY, 26, 1864.

a Pleasent time very stormy raining all day i went out in the afternoon but did not get far vincent was about as usol I went down to school but did

TUESDAY, 27.

Not stay Nell did not go out she had the sore throt the last Tuesday ni the year i was not well but i felt it to be my duty to go to meeting we

WEDNESDAY, 28.

had quit a Pleasent meeting few out very damp vincent called for me to go to the concert alfred was up to seele stoped a minute Nell did not Come this evening

DECEMBER, THURSDAY, 29, 1864.

very fine day i attended to considerable business in the afternoon vinc Nell and went to call on mr lively then to the lecture then to the fair[46]

FRIDAY, 30.

beutiful day sue and Nell stoped to see me i have not had a visit from sue for a long while [. . .] she spent the evening with Reading was here a long time Alf [Alfred] was i spent quite an agreeable day

SATURDAY, 31.

quite a heavy snow storm very disagreed it stoped snowing towards evening we made donation to mr gibbs this evening church was very gratefully received

45. As in 1863, Emilie elaborates on how she spent her Christmas in the memoranda pages at the end of her diary.
46. Emilie participated in a number of festivities during the holiday season,
like the concert she attended with Vincent on Wednesday and the fair she attended on Thursday. "City Notices," *Christian Recorder*, January 7, 1865.

Memoranda.

I Paid 5.0 ct for mary [. . .] for the organ I Promised to go to the sisters to sew [. . .] thester with neal I must get some hair[. . .] mrs bustle and [. . .] I owe Emm [. . .] a visit Em Johnson also I gave about [. . .] my photograph Barker has had some taken i am good for one

[. . .] married on Sunday [. . .] Jonson was to see me this afternoon she is very Pleasent

Memoranda.

June

Saturday [. . .] I visited the with mrs Wister[47] it certainly was worth going to we visited all the Principle Places of interest when i cam [came] out i had seen so much i hardly could recolect who i had seen I saw a perfect deal of handsome work but i did not see any done by any colored person there might of bin some things their [there] i did not see[48] martin was at our house on Sunday 2 July i did not see him i was up to whites

Memoranda.

I received my Dear brrothers photographs last week Saturday 16th, 1864

I must go and see mrs [. . .] hall the first oppertunity Nellie Paid me 7500 wich [which] was [. . .] did me [. . .] her [. . .] to [. . .] to [. . .] school

I must realy go and See Elizai Chester yesterday Oct 13th i commence taking lessons of mrs lively to day

---

47.   Emilie was probably arranging her employment with Mrs. Wister in Germantown; see note 14 above. Peitzman, "Lecture," 245–70.

48.   Emilie looked in vain for evidence of African American women's handiwork at the fair grounds. Encompassing some 200,000 square feet and several city blocks, Philadelphia's Great Central Fair focused attention on women's needle-work, featuring knitted socks, haversacks, quilts, and many other items produced by women in local soldiers' aid societies. Emilie's work as a seamstress and member of the LUA explains her disappointment at fair organizers' decision not to display this work. Milroy, "Avenue of Dreams," 31–33.

Memoranda.

Tuesday November 1st 1864 today has bin a great day 6000 slaves
have bine Declard free in the State of Maryaland it has Bin generaly
[. . .] had by our People the headquarters for the Colerd Troops was
butifuly illuminated the Soldiers Praded quite a holliaday al around
Nellie and i are to go to whites on Thursday nothing happens to
Prevent mrs Bayard Paid me $8 on the 17th

Memoranda.

we are to have a grand donation Party on new years eve to meet at
the hall and Proceed to mr. gibbses house
The emancipation of Maryaland was Celabrated in grand style in the
7th of December 1864 at National hall they had Seymours band and a
number of singers and several adresses everything was exellent

Memoranda.

I feel thankful that i have bin spard to enjoy another Christmas day
Christmas eve i had several friends up here we had quite a Pleasent
time Christmas being on Sunday I went to church herd a very good
sermon by one of the students from the institute in the evening foster
vincent kate and Nell Came up and we had quite a sociable time
together our Dear Pastor leaves us on the [. . .] the south i feel very
sorry to Part with him even for a short time

1865

SUNDAY, JANUARY 1, 1865.

beautiful morning very cold i feel very thankful that i have bin spard
while so many have bin called to their long hour i have bin spard to
see the beginning of of the new year[1] i spent this evening with Nell

MONDAY 2

lovely day home all morning very busy i wrote to brother and sister
yesterday and tomy to night comes off the long talked of Celebration[2]
by the banneker institute it was very grand

TUESDAY 3

Pleasent all day storming in the evening i have bin sick all day i did
not get to meeting I have not seen Nell since last night reading

WEDNESDAY, JANUARY 4, 1865.

was up he goes away today Sue was here this morning she seemes
very glad to stop in Pitty her much the Mrs. [. . .] called to see me
this evening Vincent stopped in

1. Emilie also elaborates on her New
Year's Day in the miscellaneous pages at
the end of her diary.
2. Emilie may be referring to a concert sponsored by the Financial Enterprise
Association at Sansom Street Hall on Tuesday, January 3, 1865. The Black Swan, Miss
E. T. Greenfield, performed at the concert
along with several of her students. Major
James J. Spelman, of the Shaw Cadets from
New York, performed for the first time
in Philadelphia. The *Recorder* called the
concert "a perfect success" and professed
the sentiment that "a repetition would,
no doubt, do much to create a healthy state
of musical knowledge among our people."
"Concert of the Financial Association,"
Christian Recorder, January 7, 1865.

THURSDAY 5

very damp i went down to Mr livelys had a very nice lesson I went home Mary Pearce was there i did not get [. . .] i went to [. . .] to a fair meeting

FRIDAY 6

quite dull this morning i received a letter from tomy this morning Mary Peirce taken dinner with me this afternoon

SATURDAY, JANUARY 7, 1865.

quite stormy all day raining in the morning snowing in the afternoon very cold Mr gibbs came home to day very sick Mr. White went down this morning

SUNDAY 8

fine day cold i am sory to say that we had no meeting not so much as a prayer meeting this morning Doct. Jones spoke for us in the afternoon in the evening Mr. [. . .] preched very interesting

MONDAY 9

cloudy all the morning Mary [. . .] called to see me Nell was here i went to Mr. Livelys he did not come to see me went to the practicing

TUESDAY, JANUARY 10, 1865.

raining fast all the morning it slushed toward evening i went down home then to meeting we had a very good meeting Nell did not go

WEDNESDAY 11

clear and cold the girls came for me to go to the practicing we all went up to the hall[3] it was very nice i did not go in the evening

THURSDAY 12

very pleasent i went down to Mr livelys he excused himself i did not have a lesson in the afternoon i went up to Mrs. Harriss and [. . .] at the Plobes

3. Emilie elaborates on her activities at the hall in the miscellaneous section in the back of her diary.

FRIDAY, JANUARY 13, 1865.

Mary Nell and John and i spent the evening at aunt Janes lovely day
but i have not bin out mary has been more turse today she seems
quite worried in mind i am discontent but she is more so

SATURDAY 14

very sormy has bin stormy these three Saturday i did not go out
concequently i did not see any one and i am quite Interested about
contributors for my book lonely morning only very

SUNDAY 15

winday i have bin trying to meditate and fix my mind more anything
that benefit me in future Mr fairbank Preached for us this afternoon
he was very inter

MONDAY, JANUARY 16, 1865.

esting [interesting] very pleasent quite cold I was up to see Hannah
Brown this afternoon went to Mr livelys had a very good lesson went
to see Vincent and became reconciled to each other snowing

TUESDAY 17

all day ceard [cleared] up in the evening Nell came up i went to
meeting we had quite a spirited meeting few out at Mr farbaux

WEDNESDAY 18

very cold to day i have bin quite busy all day as usal i have had very
good success with my work Nell did not get up this evening Vincent
came up and spent part of

THURSDAY, JANUARY 19, 1865.

very cold i went down to Mr livelys had a very nice lesson in the
afternoon i went out with [. . .] stoped at Elizas and Nell and i went
down To bustils we spent Quite an agreeable evening with Mary
Vincent

FRIDAY 20

was there clear and calm Mary came up and spent the day with me
i looked for Vincent but he did not come Nell has not bin up here to
stay any time this year

SATURDAY 21

very stormy all day i did not get home as I intended

SUNDAY, JANUARY 22, 1865.

cloudy very bad walking i went to church morning and afternoon
stoped to belle robisson Vincent come up and spent quite agreeable
evening Nell did not go out when it was not my [. . .]

MONDAY 23

very wet and rainy the streets allmost impassable i went to mr livelys
then to school we had a very nice school two new members

TUESDAY 24

very cold but clear meeting at Mrs Thomases not many out Mr gibbs
very sick Mr Derrickson quite sick

WEDNESDAY, JANUARY 25, 1865.

clear and bitter cold the rev martin lectures[4] to night i expected to go
but was disappointed Vincent [. . .] could not go Nell did not go

THURSDAY 26

exceedingly cold i went to Mr livelys had a very nice lesson in the
after noon we went up town we spent quite a Pleasent time we came
down in the cars very cold this

FRIDAY 27

morning [. . .] Alfred went over to see Frank he stoped and brought
me my rings Nell was up in the afternoon she seemed quite dull

4. Emilie may have intended to
attend a lecture hosted by the Social, Civil,
and Statistical Association of the Colored
People of Pennsylvania. Rev. James Sella
Martin, a "truly eloquent" orator, spoke
before the association on January 25 at
Concert Hall in Philadelphia. Rev. Martin
lectured on the "friends of the Union in
England," and the Black Swan performed.
The *Recorder* concluded that Rev. Martin's
lecture "stands second to none of the previous addresses made during the winter."
"Rev. Sella Martin," *Christian Recorder*,
January 21, 1865; "Rev. S. Martin," *Chris-
tian Recorder*, February 4, 1865.

SATURDAY, JANUARY 28, 1865.

last evening i went to hear John Smith read[5] Vincent taken me i was
quite delighted but i cought a severe cold from wich i have bin sick
to day

SUNDAY 29

beautiful morning not quite so cold my hand is aching badly i can
hardly write in the afternoon i went to church Doct Jones speak Ellen
treated me very cool what from i

MONDAY 30

cant Define quite Pleasent my side is very painful this morning i was
not able to go out this evening Vincent ever constant stoped after
school

TUESDAY, JANUARY 31, 1865.

very damp all day i had bin quite sick all day in the evening i waited
patiently for Ellen to up to go to meeting but she did not come i went
out we had quite a nice meeting

WEDNESDAY, FEBRUARY 1

clear and cold i have bin home all day Ellen stoped a little while
Vincent was up Phery was here we had quite a sociable chat

THURSDAY 2

quite pleasent i went down to Mr livelys spent the last part of my
time at home in the evening we spent with Mary B

FRIDAY, FEBRUARY 3, 1865.

quite pleasent all day Ellen went to have her Potographes taken
Vincent came up and spent all the evening with me he is quite constant

---

5.   Emilie may have heard John
Smith deliver his first public reading as a
demonstration of his educational attain-
ment and ability. An advertisement in the
Recorder described another student's first
reading: S. Morgan Smith read "selections
from Shakespeare, Whittier, and some
others of our best poets." The article mentioned future readings by "Mr. J. Henry
Smith and Mr. S. Morgan Smith"; the
former may have been the same John
Smith that Emilie heard read, perhaps an
ICY classmate. "Reading in Concert Hall,"
Christian Recorder, March 18, 1865.

SATURDAY 4

rather stormy in the morning Mary stoped in the afternoon in the
evening i went down home i have not bin out for some time on
Saterday evening

SUNDAY 5

clear but very blustry i went to church in the morning Mr olstin spoke
in the afternoon Vincent came up in the Evening he was very kind
And affectionate

MONDAY, FEBRUARY 6, 1865.

very fine day i went as usal to Mr livelys then to schoool we had
quite a nice lesson after the lesson i went to the [. . .] sewing we had
a good time i had to march

TUESDAY 7

very stormy Ellen was up quite a while in the morning It stormed so i
did not get to meeting Vincent came up to say good by he started for
harrisburg[6] at 10

WEDNESDAY 8

clear and cold the convention sets this morning i sent a letter to tomy
to day and wrote to liz Nell did not get up the walking is bad

THURSDAY, FEBRUARY 9, 1865.

rather better walking than yesterday too cold to go to germantown
i went to Mr livelys spent the afternoon at home in the evening Nell
and i called on Mr Jontson

6.   Vincent likely traveled to Harrisburg to attend the convention of the
Pennsylvania State Equal Rights League
on February 8. The *Recorder* implored
readers to "[c]ome from your mountain
homes—come from your valleys, and
organize for united action. The franchise,
the interest of the colored soldier, the
means and manner of education in our
State, demand our earnest and undivided
attention." The article named as organizers of the convention Jonathan Gibbs,
Emilie's pastor; Jacob C. White Jr., the
principal of Roberts Vaux Primary School;
and Alfred Green, whom Emilie mentions
on September 24, 1864. Emilie elaborates
on these events in the miscellaneous section of her diary. "Call," *Christian Recorder*,
December 17, 1864.

FRIDAY 10

we spent the evening with beck very blustery i sent my book to
Maggie [. . .] Nell stoped here this afternoon we had an old time chat
about matters and things

SATURDAY 11

clear and cold very busy all day i did not go home this evening i was
not very well Vincent i have not seen yet

SUNDAY, FEBRUARY 12, 1865.

quite a heavy snow storm this morning I hope it will not Prevent me
from going to church this afternoon i did not get to church all day
i went home in the afternoon found Vincent there they all scolded

MONDAY 13

me for ventureing out clear and cold i went down to Mr livelys then
to school Mr lively did not come after school i went to the sewing
and we had quite a nice time Ellen treated

TUESDAY 14

me very Cool i cant under stand strong [. . .] meeting up at whites
Mary and i went up very good meeting more than expected

WEDNESDAY, FEBRUARY 15, 1865.

very stormy both snowing and raining very hard walking to day Ellen
did not get up the celebration was Postponed indeffinately

THURSDAY 16

clear but very windy i went down home Ellen went to see Mr gibbs
he was much better in the evening we went to hear Fredrick Duglass[7]
very interesting

7. Frederick Douglass spoke before
the Social, Civil, and Statistical Association on February 16, 1865, in Concert
Hall. Douglass lectured on "equality before
the law" and kept the large mixed-race
audience "spell bound" for two hours.
After Douglass's address, the Black Swan
sang, accompanied by two other vocalists.
Emilie's pastor, Jonathan C. Gibbs, served
on the committee that organized the
Douglass lecture and others in the series.
Emilie also attended the next lecture in
the series, given by Frances Ellen Watkins
Harper on February 27. "Fred Douglass,"
Christian Recorder, February 11, 1865;
"Frederick Douglass' Lecture," *Christian
Recorder*, February 25, 1865.

FREDERICK DOUGLASS,

Will deliver the THIRD LECTURE OF THE COURSE before

The Social, Civil and Statistical Association

OF THE COLORED PEOPLE OF PENNSYLVANIA,

On Thursday Evening, Feb'y 16th,

IN CONCERT HALL.

SUBJECT,

"EQUALITY BEFORE THE LAW."

MISS E. T. GREENFIELD, the celebrated "BLACK SWAN,"
and the Post Band from Camp Wm. Penn, will perform
on the occasion.

[The Piano to be used, being one of DECKER BROS.', from W. J. COCHRAN,
908 Chestnut Street.]

ADMISSION TWENTY-FIVE CENTS.

For the benefit of Freedmen, Sick and Wounded Soldiers, &c.

The subsequent Lectures will be by Mrs. F. E. WATKINS HARPER,
Monday Evening, February 27th, J. MERCER LANGSTON, Esq , Thursday
Evening, March 9th, and HON. W. D. KELLEY, evening not fixed.

So far, these Lectures have been entirely successful ; the audiences have
been large and appreciative, and the Speeches highly entertaining ; with
charming Music at the opening and close, by the great vocalist Miss E. T.
Greenfield. All this has been highly gratifying to the Committee, especially
as in instituting this course of lectures, they ardently hoped by succeeding,
that they would be instrumental, not only in affording a rare and interesting
entertainment, but would actually remove much prejudice, and promote mea-
surably the cause of freedom and equal rights. Therefore, the Committee
would further impress it upon the friends of freedom, to give this movement
their presence and encouragement. Let the Hall be crowded on each evening.
They hardly think it necesssry, however, to urge the public to go hear
Mr. Douglass' great Lecture, on "Equality before the Law," as it seems obvious
that all his old and new admirers will want to hear him ; remembering his
surpassing eloquence and power ; his late flattering reception in Washington
and Baltimore ; and also the fact that new stimulus will be added to his gifts
by what Congress has just effected in passing the Constitutional Amendment,
by which universal emancipation is to be brought about in this country.

COMMITTEE.

Isaiah C. Wears,	Stephen Smith,	S. M. Smith,
U. B. Vidall,	Redman Faucet,	C. H. Bustill,
J. C. White, Sr.,	Wm. P. Price,	Henry Gordon,
Jonathan C. Gibbs,	Maurice Hall,	J. C. Bustill.

WM. STILL,

Chairman of the Committee of Arrangements.

FIGURE 17   Poster announcing a lecture by Frederick Douglass. Emilie attended
several of Frederick Douglass's lectures. This one was part of a series, with subsequent lectures delivered by Frances Ellen Watkins Harper and William Kelley.
Broadside publicizing lecture by Frederick Douglass (DAMS 11096), Leon Gardiner
collection of American Negro Historical Society records [0008], box 13G, folder 1,
Historical Society of Pennsylvania.

FRIDAY 17

quite Pleasent to day i went over to see [. . .] but did not see her
Vincent came up and spent quite awhile i reeived a note from Ellen
this afternoon

SATURDAY, FEBRUARY 18, 1865.

This is my birthday i feel thankful that i have bin spared so long i
should indeavor to debate my time in future move to the servis of my
maker with his help

SUNDAY 19

very fine day i went down to Church very few out Mr White held
forth not very [. . .] i did not go out in the afternoon this evening
i have had a very solem enjoyment with Vincent

MONDAY 20

beautiful day i was out in the afternoon a little while in the evening
i went down to school did not stay long the sewing was at our house

TUESDAY, FEBRUARY 21, 1865.

i had quite a nice circle Clear not very well to day Nell stoped in the
after noon i told her about Vincent we went up to meeting we had
quite a cheering meeting

WEDNESDAY 22

lovely bright day not very well i have something like the rheumatism[8]
busy all day hannah Brown stoped to see me John Sismson has
enlisted i was quite Disappointed this evening i expected Vincent he

THURSDAY 23

did not come raining i entended to stand for our Potographes this
morning i did not go anywhere untill evening we went to Shiloh[9]
they very interesting meetings there

8. According to a period medical reference book, symptoms of rheumatism included inflammation, limited joint mobility, aching or soreness, and fever. Today this condition is usually referred to as arthritis. Wood, *Treatise*, 468–82.

9. Founded in 1842 by Rev. John F. Raymond, Shiloh Baptist Church, located near the corner of Clifton and South Streets, was the home church of prominent abolitionist and black minister Jeremiah Asher. Catto, *A Semi-Centenary Discourse*, 109; Asher, *Incidents*, title page.

FRIDAY, FEBRUARY 24, 1865.

nearly all the Sabbath shool children are serious lovely morning
i went to have my expresssion saved i had quite a Promenade on
Chesnut St Vincent came up in the evening he seemed quit

SATURDAY 25

ansious about the Draft lovely morning quite like Spring in the
afternoon it comenced raining and rained hard all the evening
Concequently i did not get to Pay usal Saturday nights visit

SUNDAY 26

very cloudy this morning i did not go to church in the morning
Dr Jones Preached an excellent Sermon in the afternoon in the
evening i taken tea with Mr and Mrs foster

MONDAY, FEBRUARY 27, 1865.

at Nells then went to church Shiloh very Pleasent to day Nell has
the sore throat no school this evening i went to the lecture[10] very
interesting

TUESDAY 28

the last of winter we had a little snow and a little rain we have had
a very serene winter meeting at the Derricksons very good meeting
af ter meeting i went

WEDNESDAY, MARCH 1

to the sewing circle Pleasent this morning Nell is quite sick with her
Throat very busy all Mary Wilson was married this evening

10. Frances Ellen Watkins Harper delivered the fourth lecture for the Social, Civil, and Statistical Association on February 27, 1865, at Concert Hall. According to the *Recorder*, Harper delivered a ninety-minute lecture titled "The Cause and Effects of the War" before a "very large and intelligent audience." After Harper's lecture, a band of colored soldiers from Camp William Penn struck up the patriotic tune "We'll Rally Round the Flag, Boys," which elicited cheers for the Union and Harper. "Mrs. F. E. Watkins Harper," *Christian Recorder*, February 25, 1865; "The Lecture at Concert Hall on Monday Night," *Christian Recorder*, March 4, 1865.

Frances E. W. Harper.

FIGURE 18   Frances Ellen Watkins Harper. Emilie declared the lecture delivered
by poet and activist Frances Ellen Watkins Harper to be "very interesting." Photo
from Harper, *Poems* (Philadelphia: George S. Ferguson, 1900), frontispiece. Manu-
scripts, Archives and Rare Books Division, Schomburg Center for Research in Black
Culture, The New York Public Library, Astor, Lenox and Tilden Foundations.

THURSDAY, MARCH 2, 1865.

raining fast this morning i went Down to Mr livelys it comenced
raining before i got home i went up and got my Potos they are very
good I did not get far from home to day

FRIDAY 3

still raining Ellens Throat is better i Fear mine is getting soare i had not
seen anything of Mary since Monday Vincent spent the evening with me

SATURDAY 4

he is very affectionate the grand celebration[11] of the union league
came off last night very well attended rainey this morning clear in the
evening i went home

SUNDAY, MARCH 5, 1865.

lovely morning i did not go to church i Deprived myself to let lizzie
go in the the afternoon the interresting servis of Communion token
Place Nell was sick and did not get

MONDAY 6

there Vincent came up in the evening spent quite a Pleasent time
i went to Mr livelys and to school then to the circle Nell was not able
to be out very few at school very

TUESDAY 7

fine day nell is still not able to be out her Throat is very bad meeting
at bustils

WEDNESDAY, MARCH 8, 1865.

beautiful morning Ellen better it comenced raining in the afternoon
very busy making Marys wedding dress sewing untill after 1 oclock
the beautiful

11. The Union League celebration
to which Emilie referred likely was held
at Concert Hall in honor of the recently
passed constitutional amendment to
abolish slavery. According to the *Recorder*,
the Colored People's Union League Association's celebration promised music under
the direction of William A. Burris and
lectures by several prominent speakers,
including John S. Rock, a doctor, abolitionist, and the first African American
lawyer admitted to the bar of the Supreme
Court of the United States. "Grand
Demonstration," *Christian Recorder*, February 25, 1865.

THURSDAY 9

day has arrived this is Marys wedding day very rainy all the morning the sun afterard for alittle while cloudy all the evening Mary looked lovely very changeble

FRIDAY 10

all day the groom called on me this morning in company with Vincent he looked sober i went down to see Mary has quite a

SATURDAY, MARCH 11, 1865.

holaday all day Poor nell she cant enjoy any of the fun Vincent was up last night i stoped at Mrs Simsons She was out [. . .] stop at [. . .]

SUNDAY 12

lovely morning baptising at Shiloh to go under the water all children Mr. harris oftenness spoke for us this afternoon in the evening Nell gorge and i took tea with Mrs Simson spent quite a Pleasent evening

MONDAY 13

except Vincent he was not well lovely Day i had several calls the [. . .] was here and nell Mary P i met with a Disappointment in the evening we did not [. . .]

TUESDAY, MARCH 14, 1865.

school good many out very fine Day Mary was here she had bin out buying her outfit meeting at Mrs Hills very good meeting after meeting we stoped at Rachels [. . .] came home with me

WEDNESDAY 15

very fine Day nothing of note happening Mary was up and spent the evening she goes to Camp tomorrow i am sorry to say Vincent not about

THURSDAY 16

very fine day i went to Mr livelys then to school we did not have any lesson i did not go to the circle it being late when school

FRIDAY, MARCH 17, 1865.

let out quite like Spring Nell came up and spent the afternoon with me [. . .] then Vincent came up and spent the evening with me Hannah brown stopped

SATURDAY 18

a few minutes to see me i have Pain in my side again i received Tow [two] letters from Tomy and his Picture i was home this afternoon

SUNDAY 19

lovely morning i went to church Mr gibbs Preached a Powerful sermon he leaves[12] us this week in the afternoon an Indian from

MONDAY, MARCH 20, 1865.

west spoke for us Vincent was up [strikethrough] last evening bin dry nothing of interrest going on i went to mr livelys as usal very interresting lesson at school few out only one man Pleasent

TUESDAY 21

to day busy as usal Horrace Greely lecture[13] to night meeting at rachels to night very feeling meeting mr guy spoke very solem mr. gibbs started last night

WEDNESDAY 22

quite changeable to day [. . .] brown stoped in this morning Em [. . .] see Judge Kelly lectures to night Vincent stoped after the lecture[14]

---

12. Emilie's pastor, Jonathan C. Gibbs, left Philadelphia to go to the South to set up schools and to minister to the newly freed populations. Emilie elaborates on the contents of Gibbs's sermon in the miscellaneous section at the end of her diary. Richardson, "Jonathan C. Gibbs," 363–68.

13. Horace Greeley spoke at Concert Hall on March 21, his first visit to Philadelphia in six years. Greeley delivered a lecture titled "Self-Made Men." "Horace Greeley," *Philadelphia Inquirer*, March 15, 1865.

14. William D. Kelley, a judge and Republican congressman from Philadelphia, delivered a lecture titled "The War and the Rights of Humanity" before the Social, Civil, and Statistical Association on March 22, 1865 at Concert Hall. As with several other lectures, the Black Swan provided musical entertainment. Emilie does not indicate that she attended Kelley's lecture. "Lecture," *Christian Recorder*, March 18, 1865; "An Address by Hon. Wm. D. Kelley—An Interesting Occasion," *North American and United States Gazette* (Philadelphia), March 23, 1865.

FIGURE 19 William Kelley. Although Emilie attended the previous two lectures in the Concert Hall series sponsored by the Social, Civil, and Statistical Association of the Colored People of Pennsylvania, she seems not to have been present at William Kelley's lecture. Photo courtesy of the Library of Congress.

THURSDAY, MARCH 23, 1865.

he is very affectionate Plesent i went to Mr livelyes he was sick i did
not take my lesson i went out shoping met with good success in the
evening we went to hear JCs lec

FRIDAY 24

ture [lecture] he lectured very well i bout my shoes yesterday Mary
went to Camp yesterday Nell Promised to come up but did not come
[. . .] Vincent come after the lecture he is quite [. . .]

SATURDAY 25

cloudy Mary was here shoping as usal Nelly was here a minute she is
bonnet hunting i stoped home a bit while took my bonnet

SUNDAY, MARCH 26, 1865.

very raw and cold this morning i did not go to church in the morning
we had an excellent sermon in the afternoon quite a number out
i take them with me Vincent come on down & we went home and

MONDAY 27

spent the rest of the evening Vincent has enlisting on the brain i very
nice lesson this evening quite a good school after school i went to the
[. . .] sewing keep Vincent waiting a half houre

TUESDAY 28

in the cold he was very amible [amiable] i [. . .] him walking a great
deal to day went to meeting after meeting i went to Mary

WEDNESDAY, MARCH 29, 1865.

I feel quite excelent this morning i had conciderable before me to do
after i was done ironing i went down to Mary Proyders Nell did not
come up this evening

THURSDAY 30

raining all Day very disagreable i had a great deal of walking to do
i did not go to mr livelys Nell and went to Madyalene Sotts in the
evening we want to hear the lecture

FRIDAY 31

Sarah Shim was there looking like Sarah Thomas very wet and Disagreable all day Vincent came up about the eleventh hour

SATURDAY, APRIL 1, 1865.

lovely morning home all Day in the evening i went Down home Nell and went out shoping EJ is quite sick with a cold

SUNDAY, 2

beutiful morning i went to church we heard a very good Discours from one of the Students in the after noon Dr Jones held forth Vincent ever constant was up in the evening

MONDAY, 3

beutiful day i have bin quite busy all day in the afternoon i went down to Ellens to rejoce over the good newes[15] Richmond has fallen

TUESDAY, APRIL 4, 1865.

the city is wild with excitement flags are flying everywere busy day i have bin running errands in the evening i went to meeting at mrs gibbs

WEDNESDAY, 5

we had a lovely meeting quite a number out Cloudy to day home all day Nell come up in the evening we had quite an old time

THURSDAY, 6

This morning i went to mr livleys in the afternoon i Prayed very long to [. . .] visit to Germantown quite a Pleasent visit

FRIDAY, APRIL 7, 1865.

in the evening i went to [. . .] Sarah Shimes Vincent brought me my ring last night it is very hansome raining all day i was out shoping Vincent here in the evening

15. On April 2, 1865, Confederate General Robert E. Lee ordered the final evacuation of Richmond and Petersburg, Virginia. On April 3, 1865, the *Inquirer* published special dispatches dated April 1, 1865. They stated, "all anxiously look for the final and complete overthrow of the Rebel army, and the capture of Richmond *in less than three days*." The 6th and 22nd USCT served at the siege of Petersburg; both were mustered in at Camp William Penn. "Washington. The Glorious Victory of Last Week," *Philadelphia Inquirer*, April 3, 1865. Gladstone, *Colored Troops*, 109, 116.

SATURDAY, 8

lovely day i have bin out several times this morning i stoped home this evening EJ is still [. . .] Nell and went shoping as usol

SUNDAY, 9

Plesent but cool i did not go to Church in the morning in the afternoon mr adams preached for us i spent the evening at home

MONDAY, APRIL 10, 1865.

raining all day in the evening it [. . .] off [. . .] i went to mr livelys he did not come to school egerton come up here with Ellen

TUESDAY 11

quite pleasent i have bin very busy all day this evening i was too tired to go to meeting Vincent did not come up this evening

WEDNESDAY 12

this has bin quite a stressing week very [. . .] mrs Jones [. . .] i have bin with him [. . .] to get my Dress done

THURSDAY, APRIL 13, 1865.

very Pleasant Miss Janice started for Baltimore this morning in Concequence i did not get to the [. . .] al lesson spent most of the evening home

FRIDAY 14

to day is the day we Celebrate the soldiers Parrade[16] a flag was presented to the reggiment by the banneker very Plesent it every body seemed to have a holiday

16.   On April 14, 1865, the city celebrated the raising of the American flag over Fort Sumter with demonstrations as well as decorations. The 24th USCT left Camp William Penn and proceeded to Broad and Locust Streets, halting at Independence Hall, where they were presented with a flag. Octavius Catto and Jacob C. White spoke, and Lieutenant Colonel Trippe accepted the flag on behalf of the regiment. "City Intelligence," *Philadelphia Inquirer*, April 15, 1865; Dubin and Biddle, *Tasting Freedom*, 320–21.

SATURDAY 15

very sad newes[17] was received this morning of the murder of the
President the city is in deep mourning we had a meeting of the
association

SUNDAY, APRIL 16, 1865.

it Decided to PosPone the fare[18] very fine Day everyone seems to
Partake of the solemnity of the times Docto Jones spoke for us

MONDAY 17

to day was set aPart for a general holiday but seemes to me a day of
mourning i went to mr livelys then to school mr ling was not very
lively

TUESDAY 18

nothing special on home to day meeting at night not good meeting
after meeting Nell and went to Sarah Shimes Vincent invisible

WEDNESDAY, APRIL 19, 1865.

to day is a general holiday the churches are open and the day has the
apperanece of Sunday the Preisedent is considered buried[19] today
i was out in the afternoon we Did not have church mr gibbs being
away Vincent was up a little while

THURSDAY 20

everything assumes a solem aspect the streets look mournful the
people more so i went to mr livelys in the afternoon i did not get far

---

17. On April 14, 1865, President Lincoln was shot by John Wilkes Booth while attending the play "Our American Cousin" at Ford's Theater in Washington, D.C. His murder was announced in Philadelphia on April 15, 1865. Emilie elaborates on the event in the miscellaneous pages at the end of the diary.

18. Emilie learned of Abraham Lincoln's death at an LUA meeting, where she and other members of the association were putting the final plans together for a fair for sick and wounded soldiers. The fair was scheduled to begin on April 17,

but after Lincoln's assassination it was postponed until May 15. *Report of the Ladies' Association of Philadelphia* (Philadelphia: G. T. Stockdale, Printer, 1865), HSP 1; "An Appeal," *Christian Recorder*, January 21, 1865; "The Fair of the Ladies' Union Association," *Christian Recorder*, April 22, 1865; "Notice," *Christian Recorder*, April 29, 1865.

19. The papers followed Lincoln's funeral train as it traveled from Washington to Baltimore, then to Harrisburg, before arriving in Philadelphia. "From Washington," *Daily Age*, April 19, 1865.

from it rained all the afternoon and evening i spent the evening with Nellie

FRIDAY 21

cloudy and very dark the funeral Prossion Pass through tomorrow i have not bin out to day i am tired of the st Vincent was up this evening he is so full of business

SATURDAY, APRIL 22, 1865.

lovely morning to is the day long to be remembered i have bin very busy all morning the President comes in town[20] this afternoon i went out about 3 in the afternoon it was the gravest funeral i ever saw

SUNDAY 23

the coffin and hearse was beutiful this morning went down to see the President but could not for the crowd mr robinson spoke for us in the afternoon very interesting sermon after church Vincent and i tried to get to see the President

MONDAY 24

i got to see him after waiting tow [two] hours and a half it was certainly a sight worth seeing very Pelesent i did not go to mr lively we went to the concert[21] it was very nice with one exception lizzie brown sung

TUESDAY, APRIL 25, 1865.

miserable the rest done well very good house very fine day i stoped at mr Jonsons a little while Nellie and i went to see Sarah Shim then to meeting very good meeting after meeting went down town

20. On April 22, 1865, the body of President Lincoln was escorted by a military and civic procession to Independence Hall in Philadelphia. Emilie also notes this event in the miscellaneous pages at the end of the diary. "Our Dead President in Philadelphia," *Philadelphia Inquirer*, April 24, 1865.

21. Emilie may have attended the "amateur concert" put on by the LUA. "Notice," *Christian Recorder*, April 22, 1865; "The Amateur Concert," *Christian Recorder*, April 22, 1865.

FIGURE 20   Lincoln's funeral procession. Here, the procession is making its way down Broad Street on Saturday, April 22, 1865. Emilie tried twice—the second time, she waited for two and a half hours—to see the body of President Lincoln lying in Independence Hall. When she did, Emilie declared it "a sight worth seeing." The Library Company of Philadelphia. Photo: Schreiber & Sons.

WEDNESDAY 26

quite warm to day i have soore throat as a [. . .] Sunday adventure nothing of intrest to day Nell come up this evening she has not spent an evening with me for some time

THURSDAY 27

very much like summer today very Plesent i went down to mr livleys in the afternoon Nell i went out shoping i went down to bustles a little while in the evening i spent at home

FRIDAY, APRIL 28, 1865.

very Pleasent i have bin quite busy all day i expected to go to miss Dickinsons lecture[22] but was Disappointed Vincent could not go he come up in the evening as usal

SATURDAY 29

busy as usol the city is not in such a stire as it was last week i did not get out this evening it commenced raining about Dark sue was here this morning

SUNDAY 30

beutiful morning after the rain i went to church we had prayer meeting mr farbaux spoke beutifuly we had Preaching in the afternoon i stoped to see mrs gibbs Nell come up with me but would not stay Vincent was up

22. Miss Anna E. Dickinson lectured at the Academy of Music on April 28, 1865, eliciting significant coverage in the Philadelphia press. Dickinson had planned to deliver her popular lecture "Women's Work and Wages" but instead spoke of Lincoln's death, promising to donate all proceeds from the event to a fund for a permanent memorial to honor the late president. Dickinson eulogized Lincoln, noting "his love for the welfare of his fellow man, and the determination which filled his breast that freedom should be given to the millions of the enslaved within Southern soil." According to the paper, Dickinson's audience offered "[t]remendous applause" when she spoke forcefully in favor of the "right to try, convict and punish traitors wherever they may be found" and shouts of "No! no!" when she asked whether northern taxpayers should be expected to carry the burden of rebuilding the charred South. In closing, Dickinson called on the audience to remember and to emulate Lincoln as "the high water mark of American justice, liberty and mercy." "Amusements," *Philadelphia Inquirer*, April 21, 1865; "Miss Anna E. Dickinson, at the Academy of Music," *Philadelphia Inquirer*, April 29, 1865.

MONDAY, MAY 1, 1865.

quite a dull day for the first of may raining all day quite hard i heard
very good news from father yesterday this evening i stoped at
mr livelys and went down to school together not many out

TUESDAY 2

Pleasent all day the 6th regiment[23] went away this afternoon i did not
get to see John meeting at odgers quite a good number out we stoped
at Sarah Shimes

WEDNESDAY 3

quite warm i have bin very buisy Nell come up this evening Vincent
invisible this evening kate little was here yesterday

THURSDAY, MAY 4, 1865.

lovely day the examination comes off to day i did not go in
the morning i went in the afternoon very interesting after the
examination we went to the sisters Nell and i little [. . .]

FRIDAY, 5

Dull this morning i went to the alumni it was very grand i have rather
a heavy heart to day i received a letter from sister wich make me feel
quite sad this evening event of being [. . .] disapoin

SATURDAY 6

tented [disappointed] raining this morning Mary stoped here this
afternoon in the evening i went down home Ellen and i stoped at
Doct Jones

SUNDAY, MAY 7, 1865.

lovely morning i did not go out in the morning i sent a letter to sister on
Teridge quite warm in the afternoon Doct Jones spoke in the evening
i went to st Thomas[24] quite a fraciss [fracas] at millies this evening

23. On May 3, the *Inquirer* reported
that the 24th USCT had left for service
in the South the previous day. Emilie
refers to the 6th USCT, also out of Camp
William Penn, but not mentioned in the
paper. "Departure of a Colored Regiment,"
Philadelphia Inquirer, May 3, 1865.

24. St. Thomas (African) Protestant
Episcopal Church was also home to the
Ladies' Sanitary Association, the earliest
relief organization begun by women of
color to support the USCT. Catto, *A Semi-
Centenary Discourse*, 107; Giesberg, *Army
at Home*, 107–8.

MONDAY 8

raining all the morning in the evening i went to school very nice lesson after school i went to fair meeting very wet i missed Vincent had to come home by myself

TUESDAY 9

i feel very heavy all day the house in so much confusion that it woriyes me meeting at off [. . .] Nell did go after meeting nell Vincent and stoped at bustils stoped at nells

WEDNESDAY, MAY 10, 1865.

she had gone to here Nell stoped here a minute this morning she is overrun with worry i have bin working very hard all day Vincent did not get up

THURSDAY 11

clear this morning i went down home in the afternoon did not get out stoped at Sarahes it comenced raining very hard i did not get to [. . .] reidings

FRIDAY 12

[. . .] Ellen was to comes up this afternoon but did not come in the evening i went to the meeting very interesting

SATURDAY, MAY 13, 1865.

very busy all day Ellen was up this afternoon i did not get home this evening somthing unusol Sarah was quite sick this evening

SUNDAY 14

beutiful Day i went to church in the [. . .] morning in the afternoon we had a French lecture on Mr Cato comes frome in the evening i spent Pleasently at home

MONDAY 15

this is a busy day the fair[25] comences today i have bin working hard all the afternoon at the fair in the evening

25.   On May 15, the fair held by the LUA took place after a month-long postponement. The fair lasted two weeks and proceeds went to care for sick and wounded USCT soldiers. "Notice," *Christian Recorder*, April 29, 1865.

TUESDAY, MAY 16, 1865.

very busy Did not get to the fair this morning i went down home
Sarah was better sister came down this morning i went out with her

WEDNESDAY 17

she staid all night in the very busy all day i went out with anna it is
very warm in the evening we went to the fair sister went home
about 10

THURSDAY 18

quite a change in the weather quite cool i have bin at the all the
afternoon very [. . .] seeing the boys

FRIDAY, MAY 19, 1865.

warm as usol cool i have not bin to the fair to day Vincent wa[s] up
this afternoon there was quite a riot down at cleront and lombard this
evening

SATURDAY 20

between the blacks and whites quite lovely all to day i went up the
fair about 7 quite lively this evening great time sue miller was here

SUNDAY 21

quite rainy morning and a rainy day i went to church in the afternoon
bteen then prayers in the evening Professor Delany lectures at the
church i got

MONDAY, MAY 22, 1865.

very wet coming home quite cloudy all day no school the fair is all
the go now quite a good attendence this evening Vincent is home
egerton very scarce virgil about

TUESDAY 23

very busy all day i went up to the fair expecting to go to meeting but
was sadly disappointed very busy all the evening very good sales

WEDNESDAY 24

i am all most worn out very busy to day i did not go to the fair untill
evening i have not bin shoping since Sunday Sarah was up

THURSDAY, MAY 25, 1865.

to the fair go today i went down home home found reab there Sarah
furious at neli mills grand explosion on hand very busy this evening sales

FRIDAY 26

Pretty good [. . .] Plenty every thing Pleasant sis for to[night] night
is the grand concert it came off poorly we had a crowded house and
very well at the [. . .]

SATURDAY 27

to night i am happy to say is the final of the fair i have got a bad cold
by the opperation i was the there working [. . .] hold pos [. . .]

SUNDAY, MAY 28, 1865.

very cloudy all day i have bin quite under the weather all day out in
the morning did not go to church in the afternoon vincent come up in
the evening

MONDAY 29

quite Pleasant i have bin busy as usol i was agreeably surprised
to day last as i was going upstairs tom come walking in he has bin
discharged[26] in the evening Nell

TUESDAY 30

and i went to school only a few out meeting at mrs baliums quite a
good turn out Nell was not there

WEDNESDAY, MAY 31, 1865.

very warm all day i have bin working very tired after i was home i sat
down to concole my self with the idea i wou not go out mary black
com in for me to go to the

THURSDAY, JUNE 1

committee meeting i have had no rest for som time we realized over
1000 clear [. . .] the fair melting warm to day i have bin packing
away my winter clothing spent the evening at blakes

26. The Grand Review of the Armies
occurred in Washington, D.C., on May 23
and 24, 1865. The last substantial Confederate forces surrendered on May 26,
1865. Discharge of soldiers began after the
review. "The Latest News by Telegraph:
The Grand Review," *Daily Age*, May 24, 1865.

FRIDAY 2

had quite a party on a small scale i quite a nice time very warm
no prospects of my going away this summer alfred was up here a few
minutes Vincent was here

SATURDAY, JUNE 3, 1865.

very warm i have bin out in the sun a great deal Mrs Powel received
news that mrs norse was dead the hous is very mournful i was home
a minute

SUNDAY 4

Pleasent i fell very soe i will not be able to go to church to day it is
sacrement Sunday but i must learn to bear disappointment for we
meet with many in this world

MONDAY 5

to day has been a tiring day i have bin very much worried did not get
to go to school or to meeting Vincent did not stop

TUESDAY, JUNE 6, 1865.

very busy all day quite disappointed i did not get out and especily to
meeting wich i was very ansious to attend Vincent did not stop this
morning

WEDNESDAY 7

i shall be cross with him when he comes another busy day
mrs lougund come home to day she looks badly i ran home a minute
this evening alfred is quite sick

THURSDAY 8

i have no had time to answer sisters letter it rained very much but i
cant before it i went down home a few minutes in the evening

FRIDAY, JUNE 9, 1865.

very busy puting away the light clothing raining very hard in the
morning Vincent come down he is ever constant

SATURDAY 10

quite Pleasant i have bin out shoping Nell was here a minute i stoped home a few minutes

SUNDAY 11

lovely day i went to church in the morning mr gibbs Preached in the afternoon we had a scotchman he spoke well home in the evening Vincent short

MONDAY, JUNE 12, 1865.

quite warm busy all day as usal in the evening i went down to school mr lively did not come after school Nell and i went out to the meeting at mrs adams

TUESDAY 13

we had quite an exciting meeting [. . .] very Pleasently nothing of inters to day Fary was up and stayed a long time meeting at EJs very good attendance not either of the Blackes out neal went

WEDNESDAY 14

to elexander yesterday went to committee this morning i went out with Sarah and mrs adams to Purchace things for the soldiers[27] we met with

THURSDAY, JUNE 15, 1865.

good success very Pleasent we started about 1/3 ps [past] nine for the [. . .] the boat left at ten we had a Pleasant trip up the river around at white hall about 12 i shall

FRIDAY 16

ever remember white hall[28] oh we did not get time to Distribut the things as we wished but we enjoyed ourselfes very much very Pleasant out to day barker was here this evening

27. Though the LUA had reorganized on February 26, 1865, to focus on the freedmen, it continued to support the USCT as well.

28. Seventeen miles up the Delaware River from Philadelphia, White Hall, located on the grounds of an old Episcopal college, served as a hospital during the war. Green, *History of Bristol*, 73.

SATURDAY 17

paid me quite a pleasent visit vincent was up his visits are mostly
pleasent i went down town to hear the [. . .] news neal arrived last night

SUNDAY, JUNE 18, 1865.

alf Brought me a letter yesterday from anna all well very fine morning
i did not go out in the afternoon i went to church mr gibbs spoke
it seemed quite natural to have him in the evening we went

MONDAY 19

to em jones and boys Browns neither of them home fine Day Mary
davisons was up hear [here] and i spent the Day in the evening i went
to school not many out mr lively did not stay long taylor and vin

TUESDAY 20

ton [vinton] were Down after school we went to docor thomases very
warm to day meeting at Blackes very nice meeting quite a number out

WEDNESDAY, JUNE 21, 1865.

very warm to day quit busy as usal

THURSDAY 22

clear very warm Nell and i went out shoping got caught in the shower
in the evening we went into Seymours Professor stirghs and the
Douglases were with the Party

FRIDAY 23

warm as ever my Prospects of being in town all summer seem very
certain at Present Vincent was up this evening he is very constont

SATURDAY, JUNE 24, 1865.

very warm Prospects of a very warm summer after working very hard
i had to Dress and go Several erands [errands] i stoped at hom[e] and
at Nells i have not bin

SUNDAY 25

out to school Saturdyes in the evening the sirvis very hot this morning
i went to church mister gibbs held forth in the afternoon was very
fine out the heat hung so great Vincent was up in the evening we had

MONDAY 26

quite a Pleasent chat about matters and things quite rainy all day we
went down to mr lively he Played for us and sang it was quite late
when

TUESDAY, JUNE 27, 1865.

we got to school school closed last night for the summer meeting
at whites curantally i did not go down to town quite a nice meeting
not many females out

WEDNESDAY 28

quite warm busy to day alf was up this morning he goes away
tomorrow he went out to see Frank to day Nell and Sarah Pirals went
with with the s[. . .]

THURSDAY 29

this is the warmest Day we have had i think lizzie eagle was by in the
evening Nell and went up to whites

FRIDAY, JUNE 30, 1865.

quite a Plesent visit we staid quite late very warm i have bin sewing
all day for the evening we had quite a thunder storm it did not seem
to cool the air here

SATURDAY, JULY 1

Vincent was here he was quite affectionate to day feels like august
very sultry i came home a few minutes and made a shower wich was
quite refreshing

SUNDAY 2

lovely morning i did not go out we had a very interesting speaker in
the afternoon liz and i went around to sarah thomases Nell was not
out all day

MONDAY, JULY 3, 1865.

she was not well vincent was i spent the evening at home very warm
i was out shoping this afternoon in the evening i went down to
Mr livelys than to the ladies union we had quite a nice meeting

TUESDAY 4

Dorsey Party out in Power this is the great day it has bin Pretty quiet
i did not go to meeting Mary Simson is quite sick Vincent came up
about 10 i went out to see the

WEDNESDAY 5

illumination it was very Pretty very busy all day i soped in to Nell
to day to say goodby to mom she goes tomorrow

THURSDAY, JULY 6, 1865.

very warm i went down to Nells and staid all the afternoon in the
evening i went down to bustills Vincent came up late i spent rather a
dull evening

FRIDAY 7

a another very warm day i think it is the warmest day we have had a
very little shower it did not do much good

SATURDAY 8

Pleasant afternoon yester day but still warm Vincent was up last night
the evening i went down hom and to Nells

SUNDAY, JULY 9, 1865.

very Pleasant this morning i went to Church Mr white exorted in the
after noon we had Preaching the Public has met with a sad loss in the Dea

MONDAY 10

th [death] of Dr Wilson²⁹ he Died yesterday at 6 o clock in the
morning lizzie sent for me this evening she is to be married on
Thursday night i went to the meeting very satisfactory Nell was the

TUESDAY 11

re [there] concluded to continue as we are untill full very Cloudy all
day tom was up here to say goodby he goes to seek his future i had a
letter from alf on

<hr />

29. According to his death
certificate, James H. Wilson died
on July 9, 1865, of acute dysentery.
"Pennsylvania, Philadelphia City Death

Certificates, 1803–1915," index and images,
FamilySearch, https://familysearch.org/
pal:/MM9.1.1/VKDM-YZQ (accessed
May 8, 2013), James H. Wilson, 1865.

WEDNESDAY, JULY 12, 1865.

Saturday meeting last night at millers very intresting Nell or Liz
was not out i received a note from my Darling today the first i have
recieved since i [. . .] very Plesent this evening not so warm

THURSDAY 13

Pleasent all day i went out shoping a little stoped at lizzies brown
sarah Shimes not at hom spent Part of the time at Nelles in the evening
i went to the wedding had a very Pleasant time Vincent did not get

FRIDAY 14

there until after the ceremony very Pleasant all day i did not go
around to see the bride Vincent came up in the evening he is very
sweet

SATURDAY, JULY 15, 1865.

I had a letter from Will last Thursday Nell was up here this morning
and ate breakfast with us wonderful in the evening i went down
home tom came home again i went to Purchase

SUNDAY 16

something for the bride very windy this morning i did not go to
church i answered alfreds letter in the afternoon we an excellent
sermon i spent quite a Pleasent evening in Nells

MONDAY 17

raining all morning church in the afternoon i stoped at the brides but
did not see her mrs Brown was in town yesterday i did not go out this
evening

TUESDAY, JULY 18, 1865.

Clear and cool i have bin busy as usal meeting at aunty nancys very
full house after meeting we went Part way home with Mrs. harding
Mr amos was at meeting from Africa

WEDNESDAY 19

Nell came up home with me after meeting Pleasent in the day and
evening we had quite a heavy shower Nell did not get up vincent has
not made his appeerence since Sunday

THURSDAY 20

night very warm in the afternoon Nell and went on a regular tour of
visits we stoped at morgans and clayes vincent did not come until late

FRIDAY, JULY 21, 1865.

quite warm all day Nell came up in the afternoon she staid Part of the
evening she ran off soon after vincent came he paid a Pleasent visit as
usal

SATURDAY 22

very warm i have bin in the Street all the morning shoping for
Mrs. Powel in the evening i went down home and to Nells

SUNDAY 23

Very Pleasent this morning i went to Church no Preaching in the
afternoon we had a Powerfull sermon Dr. Cherman[30]

MONDAY, JULY 24, 1865.

Spoke for us vincent came up he is very [. . .] very warm busy all
day in the evening i went to the annul meeting of the association
we elected[31] our old President changed three

TUESDAY 25

of our offerces very warm and very busy meeting at elises i had a hard
work to make up my mind to go but through the influence of Pap guy
i went and not regret it we had quite a nice me

WEDNESDAY 26

eting [meeting] quite a number out quite warm to day i have bin
busy Dress making this week Vincent made his appearance late this
evening

30. "Dr. Cherman" may have been
Dr. W. D. W. Schureman, an African
Methodist Episcopal Minister preaching
in Philadelphia in the summer of 1865 to
raise funds to build a church in Baltimore.
*The History of the African Methodist
Episcopal Church* noted that he "was a
remarkable pulpiteer." Smith and Payne,
History, 86, 459–61, 465.

31. The *Recorder* carried the results
of the LUA election, noting that "Miss
A. E. Mills" was elected president, "Miss
Amina Morgan" was chosen as vice president, "Miss S. L. Brown" became secretary,
"Mrs. Elijah Davis" was elected treasurer,
and ICY teacher "Miss Carrie. R. Lacount"
was appointed corresponding secretary.
"Notice," *Christian Recorder*, August 5, 1865.

THURSDAY, JULY 27, 1865.

the sun is schorching hot to day i had some shoping to do in the
afternoon i went down town and i stoped at rachels maryes bustils
and aunt Janes spent the evening with Nell

FRIDAY 28

exceedingly warm i have bin out all the morning the sun is melting
M Scott was here this evening Vincent came up late very affectionate

SATURDAY 29

not quite as warm as yesterday but warm enough i have bin out as
usal in the evening sarah did not get off

SUNDAY, JULY 30, 1865.

Very Pleasant at morning i have not bin to church i spent Part of
the time in reading the scriptures in the afternoon i went to church
mr Amos preached after Church i went up with liz i sepnt quite an

MONDAY 31

agreeable evening quite Pleasant out the ladies went away this
morning i went down home in the evening stoped at Nells

TUESDAY, AUGUST 1

very Pleasant no celebration on hand to day very busy this morning
i went down home Sarah did not go meeting at Millers very good
turn out

WEDNESDAY, AUGUST 2, 1865.

quite warm to day i have bin busy sewing all day Nell came up in
the evening gorge Freeman came in with his guitar and enlivened the
evening

THURSDAY 3

quite warm Julia and i started for torresdale this morning but did not
get off untill the af ternoon we had a serious time before we found
Mrs Brown the had to walk from

FRIDAY 4

keninston [Kensington] in the evening quite warm i went down
to Nells this morning she is thinking about going to germantown
tomorrow

SATURDAY, AUGUST 5, 1865.

Pleasent this morning we had quite a refreshing shower in the
afternoon Nell did not go to Germantown i did not go down town
this evening

SUNDAY 6

showering all day i did not go out in the morning i was not well in the
afternoon i went out to church between the Drops did evening spent
with Nell the wid

MONDAY 7

ower [widower] was there i helped to entertain him i have bin quite
sick all day vincent stoped a very few minutes this evening

TUESDAY, AUGUST 8, 1865.

quite Pleasent Nell stoped in this morning was here a few minutes
i answered maryes letter yesterday mr ashe was buried this afternoon
very large furneal i went to meeting at mr

WEDNESDAY 9

[. . .] vincent left for harrisburge[32] this morning i was out this
morning made several calles home all the evening

THURSDAY 10

not well all day i did not go out untill evening very reluctanly then
stoped at Nell staid there all the evening

---

32. Vincent likely traveled to
Harrisburg for the annual meeting of the
Pennsylvania State Equal Rights League,
held on August 9 and 10, 1865. Many of
the last names of the Philadelphia delegation in attendance—White, Bustill, Depee,
Crummill, Gibbs, Brown, Reeve, Simpson,
Bowers, Catto, Green—appear throughout
Emilie's diary. Of the forty-nine members
of the Philadelphia delegation, however,
none bears the name "Vincent." "Proceedings," *Christian Recorder*, December 2, 1865.

FRIDAY, AUGUST 11, 1865.

quite Pleasent this morning i have bin busy all the morning in the
afternoon i was quite sick i did not go to meeting i miss vincent very
much the convention made last night

SATURDAY 12

i received a letter from vincent this morning he expects to home on
monday Nell and i went to Germantown this afternoon i felt very
weak after

SUNDAY 13

i got up to the cars lovely day and and a lovely spot we are at Nell and
i taken long walk before breakfast we did not get to church we

MONDAY, AUGUST 14, 1865.

read the bible together we enjoyed ourselves fully this morning
we were up [. . .] five started for the cares about quarter of 6
we arrived home about 7 we spent quite

TUESDAY 15

an agreeable visit very Pleasent vincent did not come last night i was
so Disappointed meeting at Mrs gibsons i waited patiently for vincent
but he

WEDNESDAY 16

did not come quite Pleasent i have bin busy all day this afternoon
i took a walk stoped at bustells and the others many Places went
home and could not

THURSDAY, AUGUST 17, 1865.

get in vinccent came last night about 10 rather cloudy this morning
i ran down to Nells a few minutes vincent was here this monrning
i did not go out this afternoon

FRIDAY 18

very Pleasent i have bin sewing all the morning i went down to Nell
about 2 spent the afternoon very Pleasenttly in the evening i went to
the lecture Mr amos spoke very feelingly i was

SATURDAY 19

much Pleased with him very haz [hazy] sewing all day Nell was up
this afternoon i stoped there in the evening

SUNDAY, AUGUST 20, 1865.

very warm i went to church in the morning and afternoon also heard
a very interesting Discours with tom spent the evening at home as
usal vincent came up late

MONDAY 21

very warm busy all the morning in the afternoon i Paid several calles in
the evening i went to the meeting but we Did not have much of any

TUESDAY 22

Cloudy all the morning it comenced raining in the afternoon rained all
the evening i did not go to meeting

WEDNESDAY, AUGUST 23, 1865.

beautiful morning Nell stoped in Mary has not come up yet home all
day vincent came up and spent the evening

THURSDAY 24

quite cool Celestien mary Clay stoped here this morning on their way
to burlington Nell and i went to Mr livelys he was not home we paid
several calles i sepnt quite an agreeable evening

FRIDAY 25

at Nells very Pleasent to day home as usal on Friday vincent did not
come up concequently i was a lone all the evening

SATURDAY, AUGUST 26, 1865.

very warm all busy as usal not of not posing in an unsettled [. . .]
about matters and things mary is expected this evening Nell came up
we went for my guitar

SUNDAY 27

Lovely and clear very warm i went to church in the morning and
afternoon Pap guy spoke in the morning mr Blackburn in the
afternoon we had an excellent sermon vincent up in the

MONDAY 28

evening windy very warm i answered annas letter to day this evening
Nell april i went to Mr livelys pleasent time mary came home to day

TUESDAY, AUGUST 29, 1865.

Cloudy all morning the grand picnic came off to day i did not attend
we received the sad news of the Death of Petrson[33] this evening
Meeting at riders very happy meeting not a great many there

WEDNESDAY 30

quite warm busy as usal Jake stoped in here a minute this morning
home all day vincent was up quite late he seems quite affected about
Petersons Death

THURSDAY 31

very warm all day redding was hear this morning he looks well
i stoped at lizzes in the evening i spent the best part at

FRIDAY, SEPTEMBER 1, 1865.

Nells mary went to Em warrichs Party she looked well quite like
Summer to day Nell was up this evening vincent came up very early
spent the evening

SATURDAY 2

very warm shower in the afternoon in the evening clear i went down
home then to bustles Saw Mrs mesely from harrisburg

SUNDAY 3

very warm all day rain in the afternoon commnion in the afternoon
very solemn mood amos taken in Church lovely evening

MONDAY, SEPTEMBER 4, 1865.

exceedingly warm to day we had one of the heavyest raines[34] i think i
ever saw this afternoon it poured an hour it cleared off in the evening
i went to the meeting

---

33. Corporal Theophilus T. Peterson, Company H, 24th USCT, died in Berkville, Virginia, on August 27, 1865, after a month-long illness. He was twenty-eight years old. "Obituary," *Christian Recorder*, September 23, 1865.

34. The papers carried news of a heat wave followed by news of "one

TUESDAY 5

very warm all day in the afternoon i started for whites stoped at Nell she went up with me we stoped at rachels bustills and betties not many at meeting Mr

WEDNESDAY 6

Weighes was very gallant very warm here all day went Down to Nells went down to see marys mother

THURSDAY, SEPTEMBER 7, 1865.

[. . .] all day i went out a little while with Nell we went down to Mrs Potters and Mr Puoylers and went Joneses and Mary B[. . .]

FRIDAY 8

raining Pretty much all day little cooler i did not go to meeting not feeling very well being very warm all the evening gorge Freeman was up here

SATURDAY 9

raining Nell was up early this morning with her bonnet i went dancing in the evening i saw her freind from concord

SUNDAY, SEPTEMBER 10, 1865.

Cloudy all day i went to church mr Jackson spoke for us he spoke well in the afternoon mr more spoke for us quite a number out vincent was up he was robed on

MONDAY 11

Saturday night very warm this morning clear in the evening we had a meeting concerning the reopening of the school we decided to comence on the first

TUESDAY 12

monday in october exceedingly warm vincent up to meeting quite a large number out very interesting meeting

of the heaviest rainstorms within the recollection of the oldest Philadelphian" that lasted for more than an hour. The rain disrupted visibility as well as mobility throughout the city. Flooding was most severe along Eighth, Ninth, Tenth, Eleventh, Twelfth, Thirteenth, and Broad Streets. "A Severe Thunder Storm," *Philadelphia Inquirer*, September 5, 1865.

WEDNESDAY, SEPTEMBER 13, 1865.

not well to day busy to day the festival comes off for the children vincent down about 7 o quite a number of children and adults were thy all seemed to enj

THURSDAY 14

oy [enjoy] them selves very much i did not go out untill evening Julia and i went to hear blind Tom[35] i was much Pleased with the preformance excepting we had to sit up stairs wich made me furious

FRIDAY 15

another warm day. Poor Frank Duglass[36] died this morning or 12 o last night i went to meeting cant say it did me much good as i went to

SATURDAY, SEPTEMBER 16, 1865.

sleep Nell did not go. very few out not quite so warm as yesterday Neal came last night Sarah and Carrie did not come to night quite a Disappointment.

35. "Blind Tom," or Thomas Wiggins, was a former slave who toured concert halls performing musical numbers he learned from memory. After emancipation, Tom continued to travel with his master, who controlled all the proceeds from Tom's popular shows. A complicated figure, Tom inspired awe with his talent—performing two different songs on different pianos, while singing a third song—but he nonetheless frustrated critics for his deep loyalty to his former master. At Concert Hall, where Emilie had attended lectures by Frederick Douglass and Frances Ellen Watkins Harper, Emilie and Julia were unprepared to be asked to sit in a separate section. Emilie's complaint serves as a reminder that racism and segregation in the city remained unchanged by the war. Susanna Capelouto, "The Tale of 'Blind Tom' Wiggins," *Morning Edition*, National Public Radio, March 6, 2002; Ballou, *Autobiography*, 452–53; "Concert Hall. Tom. The Blind Negro Boy Pianist," *Philadelphia Inquirer*, September 11, 1865; Library Company of Philadelphia American Theatre Playbill Collection summary, www.librarycompany.org/mcallister/pdf/playbills.pdf; "The Colored People of Philadelphia," *Douglass' Monthly*, October 1860.

36. According to her death certificate, Frances Douglass died on September 15, 1865, of phthisis pulmonalis, another name for tuberculosis. Emilie and her cohorts might well have shortened Frances to "Frank," and at eighteen years old, Frances was likely a contemporary of Emilie's. "Pennsylvania, Philadelphia City Death Certificates, 1803–1915," index and images, FamilySearch, https://familysearch.org/pal:/MM9.1.1/JK78-G51 (accessed May 9, 2013), Frances Douglass, 1865.

FIGURE 21   Blind Tom. "Blind Tom," or Thomas Wiggins, was a talented pianist and singer. In Philadelphia, he played at a segregated venue. Photo courtesy of the Library of Congress.

SUNDAY 17

lovely bright day i was out all day both to Sunday school and to church Nell was not out all day i went out to Duglasses after church i was at bustills to supper i spent

MONDAY 18

the evening with Nell Clear this morning in the afternoon it blew up quite a storm it rained so i did not get to go to Frank

TUESDAY, SEPTEMBER 19, 1865.

Duglasses funeral beutifull morning after the rain Nell was up this morning liz stoped in the evening we went down to Mr livelys then to meeting

WEDNESDAY 20

we had a very interesting meeting last night mr amos lead connie was there very Pleasent home all day in the afternoon Nell came up spent part of the evening vincent did

THURSDAY 21

not come lovely day i did not go out untill late spent the evening at Nells vincent very lively

FRIDAY, SEPTEMBER 22, 1865.

lovely morning i have bin busy all Day in the afternoon Nell and i went out to see the Duglasses and martha m in in the evening i went to the lecture

SATURDAY 23

Sarah came home last night long looked for Com at last very much Gleefull to day i stoped home in the morning

SUNDAY 24

quite Pleasent all day i attended church all day vincent was not at church in the morning he was quite sick[37] he went home early

---

37. Vincent was afflicted with an illness or injury that made his face swell. Whatever the cause, it seems to have corrected itself by early October 1865.

MONDAY, SEPTEMBER 25, 1865.

very cloudy i went over too see mr Jonson it very [. . .] all the
morning i did not go out Vincent did not come down his face is bad

TUESDAY 26

very Pleasent to day i received a note from vincent his face was better
last night meeting at Mrs Hills few out Nell was not there vincent not
out his face not any better

WEDNESDAY 27

very Pleasent i am looking for vincent to night Nell and barber came
up vincent not out his face is much worse

THURSDAY, SEPTEMBER 28, 1865.

Pleasent to day i did not go out untill late vincent did not come down
i went around to bustles heard the news about the young widow
baker came with me

FRIDAY 29

i receieved a note for my one he is better but not able to be out home
all day liz brown stoped at the door this evening

SATURDAY 30

lovely day barker and Nell went to concordvill this afternoon i went
home this evening carrie is quite sick

SUNDAY, OCTOBER 1, 1865.

lovely morning i did not go to church in the morning i went down
to Sunday school in the afternoon vincent was out looking very Pale
he was

MONDAY 2

quite changeable today Ellen and barker came home this morning in
the evening i went to singing school very few out vincent better

TUESDAY 3

Pleasent all day meeting at ms hawkines Nell not there very good
meeting ms egerton there vincent not down

WEDNESDAY, OCTOBER 4, 1865.

very buisy ironing Nell not up vincent come up early and spent the
evening he seemed quite well

THURSDAY 5

quite Pleasent i was out very early i done some shoping and visiting
EJ come after me to come home untill morning he started for
Baltimore tonight Connie

FRIDAY 6

very sick all day i went down to the store this afternoon in the
evening i went to the lecture

SATURDAY, OCTOBER 7, 1865.

I went down to the store this morning stoped at bustiles Central
Depot finished my bonnet this morning and done several other
important things

SUNDAY 8

lovely morning i did not get to church Connie was so cross in the
afternoon we had an excellent sermon and heard E J was very sick in

MONDAY 9

the afternoon we expected him home last night he arrived this afternoon
looking very weak singing school was splendid this evening dave

TUESDAY, OCTOBER 10, 1865.

returned volenteers were then an enlivend [strikethrough] school with
therr voices very Pleasent i was home this afternoon the sick was
better not at meeting

WEDNESDAY 11

lovely day quite warm very buisy all day Nell did not come up
vincent either i spent the evening in Practicing

THURSDAY 12

very Bright to day but so blustery i did not go far from home in the
evening i went to bustils and hecks [. . .] Craige come down this
evening vincent [. . .]

FRIDAY, OCTOBER 13, 1865.

lovely morning quite cool i expected to go to the lecture this evening
but was disapponted mr gibbs is home Nell did not come up Craig
come up and spent the evening vincent

SATURDAY 14

was up very cool and Damp commenced raining in the afternoon
i was out stop at Nell had quite a long Talk withe [. . .]

SUNDAY 15

very dull i did not go out in the morning mr gibbs Preached in the
afternoon i spent quite a Pleasent evening in Nells

MONDAY, OCTOBER 16, 1865.

beutiful morning this is the grand Prade with the firemen i went to see
them had quite a fine [. . .] of them in the evening i went to school
Mr lively did not com

TUESDAY 17

very fine day i have had quite a reception at [. . .] today there have
to [. . .] here this morning meeting at mrs [. . .] quite a number out
i was very Drowsy i did not see vincent

WEDNESDAY 18

raining all Day very buisy as usual [. . .] Craige and Mr [. . .] call this
evening he is very fine looking

THURSDAY, OCTOBER 19, 1865.

Dull morning very blustry all day i did not get any [. . .] then home
out ellens spent quite a Pleasent evening Nell Was in our house [. . .]
was up [. . .] Did not come home

FRIDAY 20

the girls were here this morning liz went home this afternoon miss
harris was home now also vincent came up and spent the evening
Nell was not up

SATURDAY 21

very Bright Day very busy all day i went Down home a while in the evening EJ not very well

SUNDAY, OCTOBER 22, 1865.

lovely morning i went to church we had no Preaching very few out Dr Jones spoke in the afternoon beutiful sermon i saw our old friend [. . .] this afternoon

MONDAY 23

Pleasent to day i went out in the afternoon Nell came up before school time we had a very interesting school not as many out as last monday night [. . .] morris came home with

TUESDAY 24

me cool this morning meeting at mrs [. . .] quite a nice meeting vincent no more tonight

WEDNESDAY, OCTOBER 25, 1865.

Beutiful Day the girls and i went over Jersey to Petersons funeral[38] it was a very solemn funeral he was buried with military honors the baneker [Banneker] was represented

THURSDAY 26

very fine Day i did not get out untill late in the evening Nell and i went to bustils and aunt Janes Nell gave me a rallyin shout not spending Thursday evenings

FRIDAY 27

with her she made me feel very bad concerning the Past + Cloudy all day raining in the evening George freeman stoped in a few minutes vincent

SATURDAY, OCTOBER 28, 1865.

was up liz brown was here quite this morning i heard very discourageing news on thursday night concerning mr gibbs he is going to leave us altogeather

38. Theophilus Peterson, a corporal in the 24th USCT, died on August 27, 1865; see note 33 above.

SUNDAY 29

quit cold and windy i did not go out in the morning not well in the
afternoon mr gibbs gave a very interesting account of the freedmen
Down south i spent the Evening with Nellie

MONDAY 30

very Pleasent today in the evening i went to school and had a very
nice time [. . .] was Down

TUESDAY, OCTOBER 31, 1865.

raining all Day it cleared off toward evening i went to meeting
we had quite a refreshing time quite a number out

WEDNESDAY, NOVEMBER 1

beautiful Day last wednsdy went to a funeral this evening we are
going to Miss Coles wedding st Thomases church was litterly
[literally] Packed the guest looked beutiful

THURSDAY 2

raining all day i went down home and amused myself by unpacking
my winter clothing Nell and i went down to hecks in the evening

FRIDAY, NOVEMBER 3, 1865.

vincent was up last night he was very [. . .] cloudy this morning
comenced raining in the afternoon rained all the afternoon vincent
Did not come up this evening

SATURDAY 4

another rany Day Pouring all Day i have are not bin out since
Thursday i Did not go home this evening sue was up here this
morning she lookes badly

SUNDAY 5

very Cold and windy i went to church today mr gibbs Preach his
farewell sermon[39] this afternoon and Church is without a Pastor

---

39. Gibbs's formal separation from
the church occurred on March 2, 1866.

"Notices and Local Items," *Christian
Recorder*, March 17, 1866.

he leaves on wednesday for the south vincent was up spent quite an agreeable evening

MONDAY, NOVEMBER 6, 1865.

quite Cold very buisy all Day no school we went to see mr gibbs not home we then went to bustils then to the Trustys [trustees] meeting we had conciderable fun after wich we went to the ladies union Nell

TUESDAY 7

i am sorry to say lost her fur cape sue was here this afternoon i started for meeting but Did not get there went to see mr gibbs stayed longer than i intended

WEDNESDAY 8

we had a long talk i feel very sorry he has left us it might of bin Prevented he has bin treated rather shabily mary stoped a minute sue spent the evening

THURSDAY, NOVEMBER 9, 1865.

lovely Day i was out shoping i was very fortunate in making a good bargain got a hansom soot spent the afternoon at home and the evening with mrs simson

FRIDAY 10

Cloudy this morning quite cold nothing of intrest hapening today busy as usal Nell Did not come up vincent either i heard last night alfred was quite sick

SATURDAY 11

clear and cold this morning mele sated for harrisburg to day i stoped at Nell this evening barker was there

SUNDAY, NOVEMBER 12, 1865.

lovely morning very cold mr gibbs is in town i hope he will speak for us to Day Dr gaites spoke this after mr gibbs in the morn stoped at bustils and mr gibbs spent qui

MONDAY 13

te [quite] an agreable evening at Nells very Pleasent to day great many are going to harrisburg vincent is going sarah and [. . .] i would like to one

TUESDAY 14

of the number but i yeild to circumstances Nell was up to sue spent the afternoon with me meeting at bundys not one of the girls out

WEDNESDAY, NOVEMBER 15, 1865.

quite warm this morning the harrisburg folks arrived to Day they were quite Disapponted in the reception vincent Did not come Down

THURSDAY 16

very much like spring today Nell and i took a little Prom made several visits spent the time quite agreeably spent Part of the evening at home and Part with Nell

FRIDAY 17

very Dull this morning Tomy simson was married last night vincent Did not come up i miss him much

SATURDAY, NOVEMBER 18, 1865.

very Pleasent to Day ellen stoped in a few minutes I went Down home a few minutes then to Nells kate did not come out according to Promise

SUNDAY 19

Cloudy i went to church in the morning we went to see mis turner and aunty holys sick in the afternoon did not get to church kate came up and spent quite an agrea

MONDAY 20

ble evening very stormy all Day i went to school very good lesson very few gentlemen there

TUESDAY, NOVEMBER 21, 1865.

raining this morning i received a letter from anna this morning Alfred is quite sick EJ is very sick i have a grea deal to worry about i did not get to meeting

WEDNESDAY 22

quite [. . .] to Day very busy Nell and rachel was up i went Down
home this evening Elijah is quite ill i fell very ansious about him

THURSDAY 23

Clear and Cold i was down home a few minutes this morning EJ
better no word from A W i fell very ansious about him vincent Did
not get Down until late

FRIDAY, NOVEMBER 24, 1865.

quite Cold EJ still continues to improve Nell spent Part of the Day and
all the evening sue was in a few minutes i have bin very unhappy all
this week

SATURDAY 25

i am so worried and sick[40] i hardly know what to do i know i ought
not to give up to bad feelings i try to look on the bright side i cant
help feeling sad i try to say thiy [thy] will be done

SUNDAY 26

lovely morning not at church i went to church in the afternoon
mr girtes Preached i did not like him as well as the first time

MONDAY, NOVEMBER 27, 1865.

Clear and Cold i have not heard from Alfred as yeet i feel quite
worried about him EJ is geting slowly i went Down to school not
many out vincent not there

TUESDAY 28

rather Pleasent to day no mail from hom EJ better meeting at offerils
very few out i stoped home after meeting Colly still was at meeting

WEDNESDAY 29

Very much like snow to Day i hav not bin out [. . .] was up Nell
spent the evening with me remarkable

40. Alfred's and EJ's illnesses left
Emilie very unsettled. November was
also the anniversary of the death of her
sister-in-law, Mary.

THURSDAY, NOVEMBER 30, 1865.

Clear and Pleasent lizzie and i went to the express office the went home i received a letter to Day Alfred is still quite sick in the evening we went to conce

FRIDAY, DECEMBER 1

rt [concert] hall to see the militonina [Miltonian] tableaux[41] it was very fine very variable today not very Cold Nell and I Paid visit to Maryes [. . .] hom they looked very cozy

SATURDAY 2

Very Pleasent quite busy all Day mary was up this afternoon i went home in the evening EJ is better Alfred is still very ill

SUNDAY, DECEMBER 3, 1865.

lovely morning quite like Spring i was at church in the morning and afternoon Sally turner was received in to Church it was communion after Church Nell and i went to see miss mill we spent a happy

MONDAY 4

time with the old lady Pleasent sue was up this morning she looks like a married lady in the evening we went to school very nice lesson stoped at mayes John had her locked up and

TUESDAY 5

the key in his Poket colder than yesterday Did not go to meting Nell and i went to Mrs livelys school did not stay long

WEDNESDAY, DECEMBER 6, 1865.

Clear and Cold i sent a letter home yesterday nell was here this morning very busy all the evening vincent stoped at a late hour

41. Opened at Philadelphia's Concert Hall on November 7, the Miltonian Tableaux featured "sixty-three splendid tableaux carrying out Milton's idea of Heaven, Hell, Chaos and Paradise." Nineteenth-century *tableaux vivants* featured elaborately decorated scenes with costumed and posed but stationary and silent actors, usually women, replicating historic scenes— in this case following the stories of Satan and Adam and Eve from the seventeenth-century poet John Milton's *Paradise Lost*. The exhibit was so popular that it remained in Philadelphia until late December. "Thursday Evening, Nov. 7, 1865," *Inquirer*, November 1, 1865, 3. "Concert Hall: Positively the Last Week," *Inquirer*, December 29, 1865, 3. Hovet, *Tableaux Vivants*, 9-10.

THURSDAY 7

very rainy Day very unusal for Thanksgivin Day to be Dull i went to
hear mr Cato[42] Preach at St Marys & in the afternoon stoped at bustils
with vincent spent the eveng with Nell

FRIDAY 8

clear and cold i was Down from EJ was out a little wayes mary was
up in the evening helped me trim my bonnet

SATURDAY, DECEMBER 9, 1865.

John came up for her very cold it comenced snowing in the after noon
quite a snow storm i did not go out as usally no letter from home to Day

SUNDAY 10

Beautiful Day not Cold very mudy i went to church in the afternoon
quite a number out stoped at bustils after church spent the evening
with sue

MONDAY 11

John an gorgee behaved in theire usal style clear mary was up this
morning we went to school egerton was here

TUESDAY, DECEMBER 12, 1865.

raining all Day meeting at EJs i [. . .] have very nice meeting few
females out after meeting Nell and i went Down to mary John com up
with us

WEDNESDAY 13

Clear all Day rain in the evening mary was up in the evening John
com for her Nell did not make her appearance

THURSDAY 14

Clear and very cold we have a Donation Party for the freedmen[43]
to Day at the school i have bin at toil all the afternoon

---

42. This is likely Rev. William T. Catto,
father of Octavius Catto.

43. For two years, Emilie served on a
LUA committee whose members collected
and distributed clothing to freedmen

in Charleston, South Carolina. Emilie's
sister-in-law Sarah Davis served as LUA
treasurer. *Report of the Ladies' Union
Association of Philadelphia* (Philadelphia:
G. T. Stockdale, Printer, 1867), HSP.

FRIDAY, DECEMBER 15, 1865.

and evening still very cold Nell went to germantown this afternoon we sent the boxes to Day vincent Did not come down as i hoped

SATURDAY 16

Still very cold was out a little while this afternoon Nell did not come in to Day she is quite a [. . .]

SUNDAY 17

quite cold this morning christenfeuld spoke for as this morning mr gaites in the afternoon the church was quite clod [cold] all day

MONDAY, DECEMBER 18, 1865.

Cold and Dull school in the evening very nice lesson quite a number out

TUESDAY 19

wet and disagreale meeting at Browns few out Nell did not go stoped there after meeting vincent was down

WEDNESDAY 20

Cold i received very sad news today my Dear Brother Alfred Died[44] at 10 oclock To Day I am so Sorry i Did not get to see him

THURSDAY, DECEMBER 21, 1865.

before he Died very Cold to Day i started for harrisburg this after noon found father nell and the rest of the family i had a very sad journey

FRIDAY 22

Very Cold this Day i have looked forward to with Dead [dread] Poor Alfred was buried[45] this afternoon no one but him that knows all things knew my feeling

---

44. Emilie began noting Alfred's illness on November 10th. Alfred died on December 20 and was buried on December 22, 1865. National Park Service, Civil War Soldiers and Sailors System, http://www.nps.gov/civilwar/search-sailors-detail.htm?sailors_id=Dav0008.

45. This seems to reference Alfred's funeral in Harrisburg.

SATURDAY 23

if it is the mister will i hope i will never have another day like Yesterday very cold i have not bin out Since i [. . .] bin [. . .] and harriet

SUNDAY, DECEMBER 24, 1865.

were here last night snowing and raing very disagreable i spent the morning in reading to father spent a quiet Sunday together i hope we may spend many more such

MONDAY 25

in the evening i went to church very Dull i started for home this morning i was quite disappointed in the way i was received at home vincent ever constant was at the Depot i went

TUESDAY 26

Down home but Did not stay i spent the evening home vincent was up Nell went to hear Blind tomy very Disagreeable i have not bin out Nell stoped after meeting

WEDNESDAY, DECEMBER 27, 1865.

still dull weather i have bin very busy all day Julia very kindly helped me mary and John were up this evening vincent was here also spent quite a Pleasent evening

THURSDAY 28

raining all Day very Dull i went Down home in the afternoon spent Part of the time in nells spent the evening home quite Pleasently vincent Did not come untill late

FRIDAY 29

clear and cold the first clear Day we have had this week busey all Day sewing vincent came up in the evening

SATURDAY, DECEMBER 30, 1865.

quite a heavy snow storm i sent a letter home on Thursday mele [mail] started for harrisburg to day clear in the evening i went Down to Nells she has the soar Throat

SUNDAY 31

very cloudy this morning i went to s church very few out mr weaver
spoke for us i stoped at marys after church she looks quite comical
sailing around this year closes with many changes who knows what
the next year will be i feel very thankfull that i am alive and well Nell
and mary are bothe sick vincent spent Part of the evening with me
we went to watch meeting[46]

Miscellaneous

Jan 1 1865 mr gibbs Preached his farewell sermon to day his text was
from 2v of acts 32 verse and now brethren i commend you to god
A grand reception was given on the 11th of Jan for mr pierson the
antislavery sufferer vincent went to harrisburg on the 7th of Feb to
attend[47] the convention Feeb 20th 1865
John Simson has at last enlisted mary is quite distressed mary S maried
[. . .] the 9th 1865 an eventful wedding mr gibbs married them

Miscellaneous

March 19 mr gibbs Preached a very impressive sermon from the text
the kings bussiness requires hast som [. . .]
April 14, 1865 The President Was assasinated by Som Confederate
villain[48] at the theathre die Saturday morning the 15 the city is in the
Deepest sorrow
These are strang times The body of the President Passed through on
the 22 of april Dec [. . .] 1865 Sues boy born this afternoon i was
there in the afternoon after church

all is well that ends well
485 york avenue
439 north fourth st

46. The first Watch Night was held on December 31, 1862, as African Americans met in anticipation of the announcement of the Emancipation Proclamation. Many black churches carried on the Watch Night tradition, including the network of churches in Philadelphia's Seventh Ward. Keyes, "Watch Nights."

47. See note 6 above.

48. The "Confederate villain" to whom Davis refers is John Wilkes Booth. A native of Maryland, Booth joined the Richmond militia prior to the war and was present at the hanging of John Brown. On April 14, Booth fatally shot the president. He was captured by Union troops twelve days later. Emilie notes this event in her entry on April 15, 1865.

FIGURE 22 Last page of Emilie Davis's 1865 diary. At the end of her 1865 diary, Emilie wrote the words "all is well that ends well," followed by two addresses. Emilie Davis diary, 1865 (DAMS 4963), vol. 3 of Davis diaries [3030], Historical Society of Pennsylvania.

Coda: *All's Well That Ends Well*

Emilie's diaries end with the words "all is well that ends well" on the inside back cover of the 1865 volume. We can find faint traces of her in the records after 1865.

Emilie married George Bustill White on December 13, 1866.[1] George, a son of Jacob C. White, a prominent black businessman, was also the brother of Jacob Jr. (Jake), who co-founded the Pythians, a black baseball team, and who became principal of the all-black Roberts Vaux Primary School. According to an 1866 city directory, George and his brother Jacob Jr. lived at 485 York Avenue, their father's home. In 1867, George—and now Emilie—lived with Jacob Sr. at 439 North Fourth Street.[2] Careful readers of the diary will note that Emilie first mentions George's attending a wedding with Jake, on January 28, 1863, and on March 10, 1863, "gorge" was "very gallant." On the marriage registry, George's occupation is listed as "barber," but he was also very involved in the family business—politics. George was active in the Pennsylvania State Equal Rights League, a group that lobbied successfully in Harrisburg for state support for federal civil rights amendments and for a variety of state-level measures, such as the integration of Philadelphia's streetcars in

---

1. George Bustill White and Emily [*sic*] Frances Davis, December 13, 1866, Return of Marriages, October 22–December 31, 1866, Philadelphia City Archives.

2. *McElroy's Philadelphia City Directory for 1866* (Philadelphia, 1866), 779–80; *Philadelphia City Directory for 1867* (Philadelphia: McElroy & Co, 1867), 963.

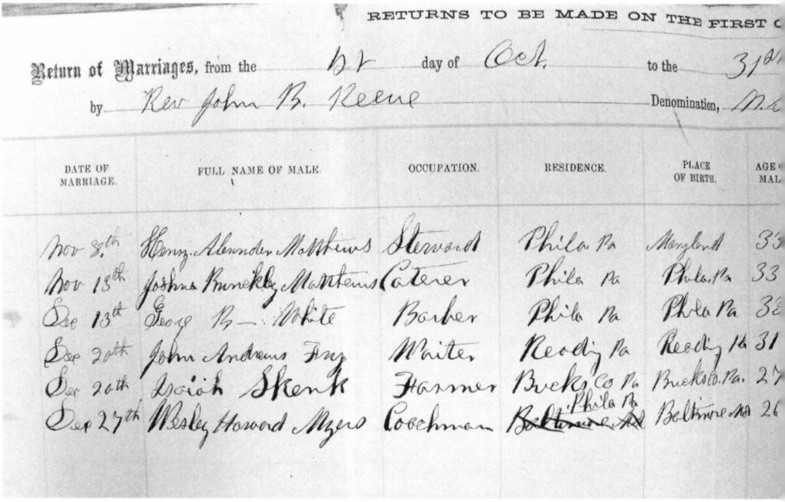
RETURNS TO BE MADE ON THE FIRST

Return of Marriages, from the 1st day of Oct. to the 31st

by Rev John B. Reeve Denomination, M

DATE OF MARRIAGE	FULL NAME OF MALE	OCCUPATION	RESIDENCE	PLACE OF BIRTH	AGE OF MAL
Nov 8th	Henry Alexander Matthews	Steward	Phila Pa	Maryland	33
Nov 13th	Joshua Brinckley Matthews	Caterer	Phila Pa	Phila Pa	33
Dec 13th	George B. White	Barber	Phila Pa	Phila Pa	3
Dec 20th	John Andrews Fry	Waiter	Reading Pa	Reading Pa	31
Dec 20th	Isaiah Skenk	Farmer	Bucks Co Pa	Bucks Co Pa	27
Dec 27th	Wesley Howard Myers	Coachman	~~Baltimore Md~~ Phila Pa	Baltimore Md	26

FIGURE 23 Emilie Davis and George B. White's marriage registry entry. Emilie married George White on December 13, 1866. Return of Marriages, October 1–December 31, 1866. Courtesy of Philadelphia City Archives.

1867. Either Emilie spelled her name "Emily" on the marriage registry or the person taking the information spelled it that way, but in any case, the new spelling seemed to stick.

Emilie appears in the 1870 and 1880 censuses as Emily F. White. (Emilie's middle name was given as Frances on the 1866 marriage registry.) The young couple wasted no time beginning their own family. Their son Jacob C. White was born the year after they were married and was likely named for George's father. (In the 1900 census, Jacob is listed as "Clement J. White," suggesting that he adopted his middle name as his first.) When Jacob was two, his mother gave birth to a girl they named Maria. Maria was followed by Emilie (b. 1873). Little Emilie's name was misspelled on the 1880 census as "Emily," but at birth she was registered as "Emilie," just like her mother. After Emilie came George (b. 1875), Carry (b. 1877), and Julia (b. 1881)—this last girl named, perhaps, for Emilie's friend in the diary (see the entry of

September 24, 1865).[3] We do not know whether more children followed, but Emilie, who was forty-two years old in 1881, may have decided that Julia would be her last child. In the 1880 census, Emilie's occupation was listed as "housekeeper," suggesting that she had achieved the status of the women for whom she used to work during those long, lonely summers in Germantown and East Falls. With five young children at home and a sixth on the way, Emilie might even have hired her own help—at least with the sewing.

In later years, Emilie contributed money to her church and rented a pew under her own name, not George's—additional indications of status that she had not enjoyed in 1863, when she was more

3. 1880 United States Federal Census, Philadelphia, Pennsylvania, roll 1173, family history film 1255173, page 10C, enumeration district 197, image 0022; 1900 United States Federal Census, Philadelphia Ward 30, Philadelphia, Pennsylvania, roll 1472, page 2B, enumeration district 0757, FHL microfilm 1241472.

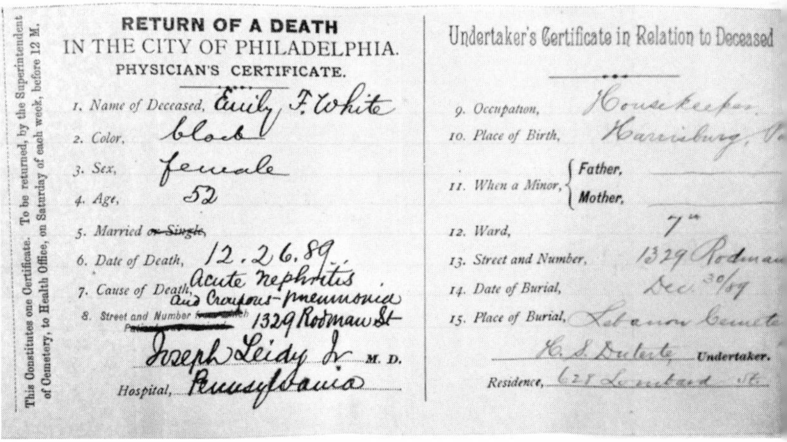

This Constitutes one Certificate. To be returned, by the Superintendent of Cemetery, to Health Office, on Saturday of each week, before 12 M.

RETURN OF A DEATH
IN THE CITY OF PHILADELPHIA.
PHYSICIAN'S CERTIFICATE.

1. *Name of Deceased,* Emily F. White
2. *Color,* black
3. *Sex,* female
4. *Age,* 52
5. *Married* ~~or Single~~
6. *Date of Death,* 12.26.89.
7. *Cause of Death,* Acute nephritis and Croupous-pneumonia
8. Street and Number ~~[illegible]~~ Patient 1329 Rodman St

Joseph Leidy Jr M. D.

Hospital, Pennsylvania

Undertaker's Certificate in Relation to Deceased

9. *Occupation,* Housekeeper
10. *Place of Birth,* Harrisburg, Pa
11. *When a Minor,* Father, Mother,
12. *Ward,* 7th
13. *Street and Number,* 1329 Rodman
14. *Date of Burial,* Dec 30/89
15. *Place of Burial,* Lebanon Cemetery

[illegible] Undertaker.

Residence, 628 Lombard St.

FIGURE 24 Emilie White's death certificate. Emilie died in 1889, at age fifty-one. Emily (Emilie) F. White, Return of Death, burial date: December 30, 1889, Lebanon Cemetery. Courtesy of Philadelphia City Archives.

concerned that someone in her boarding house had taken $7 from her than impressed by news reports announcing the Union's twin victories at Gettysburg and Vicksburg. Emilie's marriage to George Bustill White cemented her connections to Philadelphia's remarkably stable and successful black middle class.

Emilie died on December 26, 1889, just two weeks after the couple's twenty-third anniversary.[4] Although her death certificate lists her age as fifty-two, Emilie died about two months shy of her fifty-first birthday. She was buried at Lebanon Cemetery (now Eden Cemetery, in Collingdale, Pennsylvania, southwest of Philadelphia), the burial place of Octavius Catto and other civil rights luminaries of her generation. Ten years later, George joined Emilie there.[5]

4. Emilie's death certificate indicates that she was suffering from two infections at once—one in her lungs (croupous pneumonia) and another in her kidneys (acute nephritis). "Pennsylvania, Philadelphia City Death Certificates, 1803–1915," index and images, FamilySearch, https://familysearch.org/pal:/MM9.1.1/J6S3-9L6 (accessed May 10, 2013), Emily F. White, 1889.

5. George Bustill White died on June 1, 1899. "Pennsylvania, Philadelphia City Death Certificates, 1803–1915," index and images, FamilySearch, https://familysearch.org/pal:/MM9.1.1/JDT2-38D (accessed November 1, 2013), George B. White, 1899.

PRIMARY SOURCES

Newspapers
Christian Recorder (Philadelphia)
Daily Age (Philadelphia)
Douglass' Monthly (Rochester)
Illustrated New Age (Philadelphia)
North American and United States Gazette (Philadelphia)
Philadelphia Inquirer
Philadelphia Press
Public Ledger (Philadelphia)

Manuscript Collections and Online Materials
Ancestry.com and The Church of Jesus Christ of Latter-day Saints,
        Provo, Utah
        United States Federal Census data for 1850, 1860, 1880, and 1900
Department of the Navy, Washington, D.C.
        Naval History and Heritage Command, http://www.history.navy
            .mil
FamilySearch and The Church of Jesus Christ of Latter-Day Saints,
        Provo, Utah
        Philadelphia City Death Certificates, 1803–1915
Friends Historical Library of Swarthmore College, Swarthmore,
        Pennsylvania
        Association for the Care of Colored Orphans Records, 1822–1979,
            Record Group 4/008
Historical Society of Pennsylvania, Philadelphia
        American Negro Historical Society, Emilie Davis Diaries, Ladies'
            Union Association of Philadelphia, Philadelphia Female Anti-
            Slavery Society, and United States Sanitary Commission,
            Philadelphia Branch, Collections
Howard University Archives, Washington, D.C.
        Frederick Douglass, "Pictures and Progress," 1863
Library Company of Philadelphia
        American Theatre Playbill Collection

Making of African American Identity. Vol. 1, *1500–1865.* National Human-
    ities Center Resource Toolbox Library: Primary Resources in
    U.S. History and Literature, http://nationalhumanitiescenter
    .org/pds/maai/
National Archives, Philadelphia
        Camp William Penn Collection, Provost Marshal General's
            Bureau (Civil War) Record Group 110
National Park Service
        Civil War Soldiers and Sailors System database, http://www.nps
            .gov/civilwar/soldiers-and-sailors-database.htm
Philadelphia City Archives
        Death Certificates and Return of Marriages
University of Pennsylvania, University Archives and Records Center,
    Philadelphia
        Penn Biographies
University of Virginia, Charlottesville
        Historical Census Browser County-Level Results for 1860, http://
            mapserver.lib.virginia.edu/php/county.php

Published Works

Asher, Jeremiah. *Incidents in the Life of the Rev. J. Asher, Pastor of Shiloh
    (Coloured) Baptist Church, Philadelphia, U.S.: And a Concluding
    Chapter of Facts Illustrating the Unrighteous Prejudice Existing in
    the Minds of American Citizens toward their Coloured Brethren.*
    London: Charles Gilpin, 1850.
Ballou, Adin. *Autobiography of Adin Ballou, 1803–1890.* Edited by William
    Sweetzer Heywood. Lowell, Mass., 1896.
Bates, Samuel P. *History of Pennsylvania Volunteers, 1861–5.* Harrisburg:
    B. Singerly, 1871.
*The Black Swan at Home and Abroad: Or, a Biographical Sketch of Miss
    Elizabeth Taylor Greenfield, the American Vocalist.* Philadelphia:
    William S. Young, Printer, 1855.
Catto, William T. *A Semi-Centenary Discourse Delivered in the First
    African Presbyterian Church, Philadelphia, 1857: With a History of
    the Church from Its First Organisation.* Philadelphia: Joseph M.
    Wilson, 1857.
Chesnut, Mary. *Mary Chesnut's Civil War.* Edited by C. Vann Woodward.
    New Haven: Yale University Press, 1981.
Fisher, Sidney George. *A Philadelphia Perspective: The Diary of Sidney
    George Fisher Covering the Years 1834–1871.* Edited by Nicholas B.
    Wainwright. Philadelphia: The Historical Society of Pennsylva-
    nia, 1967.

Grimké, Charlotte Forten. *The Journals of Charlotte Forten Grimké*. Edited by Brenda Stevenson. New York: Oxford University Press, 1988.

McElroy's Philadelphia City Directory, 1844–1866. Philadelphia: A. McElroy & Co, 1844–66. Greater Philadelphia Geo History Network, http://www.philageohistory.org/rdic-images/index2.cfm.

Penny, Virginia. *The Employments of Women: A Cyclopaedia of Woman's Work*. Boston: Walker, Wise, & Company, 1863.

Still, William. *The Underground Railroad*. Philadelphia: Porter & Coates, 1872.

Strong, George Templeton. *Diary of George Templeton Strong: The Civil War, 1860–1865*. Edited by Allan Nevins and Milton Halsey Thomas. New York: Macmillan, 1952.

SECONDARY SOURCES

Bacon, Margaret Hope. *But One Race: The Life of Robert Purvis*. Albany: State University of New York Press, 2010.

Binder, Frederick M. "Pennsylvania Negro Regiments in the Civil War." *Journal of Negro History* 37, no. 4 (1952): 383–417.

Brumberg, Joan Jacobs. *The Body Project: An Intimate History of American Girls*. New York: Vintage, 1998.

Calderhead, William L. "Philadelphia in Crisis: June–July, 1863." *Pennsylvania History* 28, no. 2 (1961): 142–55.

Capelouto, Susanna. "The Tale of 'Blind Tom' Wiggins." *Morning Edition*, National Public Radio, March 6, 2002.

Conyers, Charlene. *A Living Legend: The History of Cheyney University, 1837–1951*. Cheyney: Cheyney University Press, 1990.

DeCaro, Jr., Louis A. *John Brown: The Cost of Freedom; Selections from His Life and Letters*. New York: International Publishers, 2007.

Dobak, William A. *Freedom by the Sword: The U.S. Colored Troops, 1862–1867*. Washington, D.C.: Center for Military History, United States Army, 2011.

Dorwart, Jeffrey M. *Fort Mifflin of Philadelphia: An Illustrated History*. Philadelphia: University of Pennsylvania Press, 1998.

Dubin, Murray, and Dan Biddle. *Tasting Freedom: Octavius Catto and the Battle for Equality in Civil War America*. Philadelphia: Temple University Press, 2010.

Du Bois, W. E. B. *The Autobiography of W. E. B. Du Bois: A Soliloquy on Viewing My Life from the Last Decade of Its First Century*. New York: International Publishers, 1968.

———. *The Philadelphia Negro: A Social Study*. Philadelphia: University of Pennsylvania, 1899.

Dunbar, Erica Armstrong. *A Fragile Freedom: African American Women and Emancipation in the Antebellum City*. New Haven: Yale University Press, 2008.

Foner, Eric. *Reconstruction: America's Unfinished Revolution, 1863–1877*. New York: Harper & Row, 1988.

Foner, Philip. "The Battle to End Discrimination Against Negroes on Philadelphia Street Cars (Part I): Background and Beginning of the Battle." *Pennsylvania History* 40, no. 3 (1973): 261–92.

———. "The Battle to End Discrimination Against Negroes on Philadelphia Street Cars (Part II): The Victory." *Pennsylvania History* 40, no. 4 (1973): 368–72.

Gallman, J. Matthew. *Mastering Wartime: A Social History of Philadelphia During the Civil War*. New York: Cambridge University Press, 1990.

———. "Snapshots: Images of Men in the United States Colored Troops." *American Nineteenth Century History* 13, no. 2 (2012): 127–51.

———. "Voluntarism in Wartime: Philadelphia's Great Central Fair." In *Toward a Social History of the American Civil War: Exploratory Essays*, 93–116. New York: Cambridge University Press, 1990.

Gatewood, Willard B. *Aristocrats of Color: The Black Elite, 1880–1920*. Bloomington: Indiana University Press, 1990.

Giesberg, Judith. *Army at Home: Women and the Civil War on the Northern Home Front*. Chapel Hill: University of North Carolina Press, 2009.

Gladstone, William A. *United States Colored Troops, 1863–1876*. Gettysburg: Thomas Publications, 1990.

Glenner, Richard A., and P. Willey. "Dental Filling Materials in the Confederacy." *Journal of Civil War Medicine* 15, no. 1 (2011): 28–33.

Green, Doron. *A History of Bristol Borough in the County of Bucks, State of Pennsylvania: Anciently Known as "Buckingham" Being the Third Oldest Town and Second Chartered Borough in Pennsylvania; From Its Earliest Times to the Present Year*. Bristol: C. S. Magrath, 1911.

Hacker, J. David. "A Census-Based Count of the Civil War Dead." *Civil War History* 57, no. 4 (2011): 307–48.

Harrold, Stanley. *Border War: Fighting Over Slavery Before the Civil War*. Chapel Hill: University of North Carolina Press, 2010.

Hovet, Grace Ann, with Theodore R. Hovet Sr. *Tableaux Vivants: Female Identity Development Through Everyday Performance*. Xlibris, 2009.

Jackson, Joseph. *Encyclopedia of Philadelphia*. Harrisburg, Pa.: National Historical Association, 1932.

Jones, Jacqueline. *American Work: Four Centuries of Black and White Labor*. New York: W. W. Norton, 1998.

Keyes, Allison. "'Watch Nights,' a New Year's Celebration of Emancipation." National Public Radio, December 23, 2012. http://www.npr .org/2012/12/29/167905308/watch-nights-honor-emancipation -proclamations-anniversary.

Labov, William. *Language in the Inner City: Studies in the Black English Vernacular*. Philadelphia: University of Pennsylvania Press, 1972.

Lapsansky, Emma Jones. "'Discipline to the Mind': Philadelphia's Banneker Institute, 1854–1872." *Pennsylvania Magazine of History and Biography* 117, nos. 1/2 (1993): 83–102.

———. "The World the Agitators Made: The Counterculture of Agitation in Urban Philadelphia." In *Abolitionist Sisterhood: Women's Political Culture in Antebellum America*, ed. Jean Fagan Yellin and John C. Van Horne, 91–100. Ithaca: Cornell University Press, 1994.

Lepore, Jill. "Historians Who Love Too Much: Reflections on Microhistory and Biography." *Journal of American History* 88, no. 1 (2001): 129–44.

Lott, Eric. *Love and Theft*. New York: Oxford University Press, 1933.

Meier, Michael T. "Civil War Draft Records: Exemptions and Enrollments." *Prologue Magazine,* Winter 1994. http://www.archives .gov/publications/prologue/1994/winter/civil-war-draft-records .html.

Milroy, Elizabeth. "Avenue of Dreams: Patriotism and the Spectator at Philadelphia's Great Central Sanitary Fair." In *Making and Remaking Pennsylvania's Civil War*, ed. William Blair and William Pencak, 23–57. University Park: Pennsylvania State University Press, 2001.

Nash, Gary, and Jean Soderlund. *Freedom by Degrees: Emancipation in Pennsylvania and Its Aftermath*. New York: Oxford University Press, 1991.

Painter, Nell Irvin. *Sojourner Truth: A Life, a Symbol*. New York: W. W. Norton, 1996.

Peitzman, Steven J. "The Fielding H. Garrison Lecture: 'I Am Their Physician'; Dr. Owen J. Wister of Germantown and His Too Many Patients." *Bulletin of the History of Medicine* 83, no. 3 (2009): 245–70.

Reidy, Joseph P. "Black Men in Navy Blue During the Civil War." *Prologue Magazine* 33, no. 3 (2001). http://www.archives.gov/ publications/prologue/2001/fall/black-sailors-1.html.

Richardson, Joe M. "Jonathan C. Gibbs: Florida's Only Negro Cabinet Member." *Florida Historical Quarterly* 42, no. 4 (1964): 363–68.

Silcox, Harry. "Philadelphia Negro Educator: Jacob C. White, Jr., 1837–1902." *Pennsylvania Magazine of History and Biography* 97, no. 1 (1973): 75–98.

Smith, Charles Spencer, and Daniel Alexander Payne. *A History of the African Methodist Episcopal Church: Being a Volume Supplemental to a History of the African Methodist Episcopal Church.* Philadelphia: Book Concern of the A.M.E. Church, 1922. Reprint, Philadelphia: Johnson Reprint, 1968.

Smitherman, Geneva. *Word from the Mother: Language and African Americans.* New York: Routledge, 2006.

Stansell, Christine. *City of Women: Sex and Class in New York, 1789–1860.* New York: Alfred A. Knopf, 1982.

Tremel, Andrew T. "The Union League, Black Leaders, and the Recruitment of Philadelphia's African American Civil War Regiments." *Pennsylvania History* 80, no. 1 (2013): 13–36.

Weigley, Russell Frank. "The Border City in Civil War, 1854–1865." In *Philadelphia: A 300-Year History,* 363–416. New York: W. W. Norton, 1982.

Wert, Jeffry D. "Camp William Penn and the Black Soldier." *Pennsylvania History* 46, no. 4 (1979): 335–46.

———. *Fort Mifflin of Philadelphia: An Illustrated History.* Philadelphia: University of Pennsylvania Press, 1998.

Winch, Julie. *A Gentleman of Color: The Life of James Forten.* New York: Oxford University Press, 2003.

Wood, George B. *Treatise on the Practice of Medicine.* 5th ed. Vol. 2. Philadelphia: J. B. Lippincott, 1858.

Theresa Altieri received her B.A. from the University of Pennsylvania in 2009 and her M.A. in history from Villanova University in 2012. She is Archivist of the Abraham Lincoln Foundation of the Union League of Philadelphia.

Rebecca Capobianco received her B.A. in history from Villanova University in 2011 and her M.A. in public history from Villanova University in 2013. She currently works at Fredericksburg and Spotsylvania National Military Park.

Thomas (Tom) Foley is a 2009 graduate of the University of Notre Dame and received his M.A. in U.S. history from Villanova University in 2013. He is currently pursuing a Ph.D. at Georgetown University.

Judith Giesberg is Professor of History and directs the graduate program at Villanova University.

Ruby Johnson received her B.A. in 2011 from Moravian College in Bethlehem, Pennsylvania, and her M.A. in history from Villanova University in 2013. She is currently a Ph.D. student in U.S. history at The George Washington University.

Jessica Maiberger graduated from Heidelberg University in 2008 and received her M.A. in history at Villanova University in 2013. She is Collections Manager at Huron Historical Society and Office Coordinator at the Rutherford B. Hayes Presidential Center in Fremont, Ohio.